Rock & Role

Rock & Role: American Rock Group Appearances on Scripted U.S. Television Series (1964–1970)

By Mike Dugo

BearManor Media

2023

Published in the USA by
BearManor Media
1317 Edgewater Dr. #110
Orlando, FL 32804
www.BearManorMedia.com

Softcover Edition
ISBN: 979-8-88771-182-9

Printed in the United States of America

This book is dedicated to my wife and the love of my life, Diane, whose belief in my writing continues to inspire me to this day;

And to my late brother, Joey, whom I think of every time I hear specific songs or watch certain TV shows. His influence will stay with me forever.

Table of Contents

Acknowledgments

Most of the research contained here within was guided by the enthusiasm of the RVSP (Rock Video Sixties Project) in the early-to-mid 2000s. Several dedicated members contributed *TV Guide* and newspaper research long before the availability of online archives; others contributed VHS and/or DVDs of the television programs referenced. THANK YOU to Ben Chaput, Gary Belich, Tom Alger, and Tom Kleinschmidt for contributing the lion's share. Other invaluable contributions were provided by Matt Hoffman, Tony Sanchez, Deena Canale and Mark Rogers.

All quotes by band members not attributed in the summaries were provided to the author during his stint as owner and operator of the now defunct website 60sgaragebands.com (2002-2015). Other contributions are credited in the individual entries. Special thanks to all the band members who graciously provided recollections, even when a response wasn't necessarily expected (and in no particular order): Larry Tamblyn (Standells), Daniel Hortter (Yellow Payges), Gary Marker (Rising Sons), Eddie Hodges, Don Grady (Greefs), Evan Zang (Paper Fortress), Don Glut (Penny Arkade), Ted Myers (Chamaeleon Church), Johnny Green (Johnny Green & the Greenmen), Danny Faragher (Peppermint Trolley Co.), George Bunnell (Strawberry Alarm Clock), Dominic Demieri (Sundowners), Susannah Jordan (Pillory), Davie Allan (Davie Allan & the Arrows), John Chris Christensen (Opus 1), George Caldwell (Bees/W.C. Fields Memorial Electric String Band), Michael Sulsona (Spats), Louis Paul, Jr. (Guilloteens), and Boomer Owen Castleman (Lewis & Clarke Expedition).

Extreme and additional thanks are in order for those resources whose research has repeatedly been invaluable over the course of several years and, sometimes, countless inquiries: Chris Bishop, Bruno Ceriotti, T. Mike, Alec Palao, and Mike Stax.

As noted in the introduction, there are undoubtedly rock group appearances that have not been uncovered yet nor documented elsewhere. If you know of any, please contact me at 60sRockTVCameos@gmail.com. All information is welcomed!

Introduction

With a reported audience of over 73 million people, the impact the Beatles' first appearance on *The Ed Sullivan Show* had on popular music is well documented. Ushering in the British Invasion, the excitement (or rather, hysteria) the Fab Four generated paved the way for other English rock groups and musical artists to visit U.S. shores, affecting national sale charts and dominating radio airplay. "Beatlemania" was everywhere, and American culture took note. Paul, John, George and Ringo's influence shaped teen hairstyles, fashion, and slang and their visages adorned an incredible array of merchandise. Their enormous popularity spawned an entire garage band revolution leading to the sales of musical instruments reaching all-time highs. With so many dollars to be had, industries of all verticals looked to capitalize. Within a year, television did so by broadcasting in prime time two shows—*Shindig* and *Hullabaloo*—devoted solely to the popular music of the day.

The precursor of all rock and roll shows, of course, was *American Bandstand*. Although it had premiered in Philadelphia in 1952 it didn't debut nationally until 1957, when it faced competition from Baltimore's *The Buddy Deane Show*. Both programs, however, were relegated to afternoon hours. Alan Freed's *The Big Beat* debuted nationally in prime time in 1957, but the first credited appearance of a rock and roll group on prime time network television was, perhaps not coincidentally, also on a program hosted by Sullivan—*Toast of the Town*—when, in August 1955, Bill Haley & His Comets performed 'Rock Around the Clock'. In November 1955, Bo Diddley appeared on *The Ed Sullivan Show*. Elvis Presley shook things up after his performance of 'Hound Dog' on *The Steve Allen Show* in July 1956, leading to an appearance a year later on Sullivan's program. Either Allen or Sullivan would feature other early rock and rollers, including Buddy Holly, Jerry Lee Lewis, and Fats Domino.

While rock and roll music performances aired during prime time hours weren't necessarily a new thing before the Fab Four's *Ed Sullivan Show* appearance on February 9, 1964, the performances were primarily limited to live acts on either variety or music-oriented shows, or fictional non-rock and roll groups portrayed by actors essaying the roles in sitcoms like *The Andy Griffith Show*. The one notable exception was *The Adventures of Ozzie & Harriet*. Ricky Nelson had played a major roll on his father's scripted television program since 1952 but secured a music career while acting on the program. In April 1957, in an episode titled "The Drummer", Nelson performed Fats Domino's 'I'm Walkin'' while sitting in with fictional group the Tommy Jackson Band (interestingly, instead of "rock and roll", the music was referred to as "rhythm and blues"). Nelson scored a string of hits during the late '50s and early '60s and often performed his latest single during episodes throughout the series until it had run its course in 1966. Many of Nelson's (and band, featuring guitarist James Burton) performances were filmed separately and simply inserted at the end of an episode by way of a simple introduction by Ozzie, who might have been seated in front of a television—or without any introduction at all. Some episodes, such as "Early Rush Party" (March 10, 1965) and "The Ghost Town" (December 9, 1965, as a country band) worked a performance in to the script, with Ricky's band playing at a party. There were approximately sixty episodes that squeezed in a musical performance one way or another, with eighteen of them being post-Beatles.

Other early scripted television programs also included musical guest stars. The Kingston Trio appeared *on Mrs. G Goes to College* in 1962 while the Lettermen performed on *Dobie Gillis* in 1963. Without question, it was the Beatles' *The Ed Sullivan Show* appearance, however, that convinced television executives—and, more importantly, sponsors—that televised rock and roll was good for ratings and, therefore, the bottom line. From 1964–1970, many scripted U.S. television programs—both comedy and drama—featured not only hit makers but also obscure local groups that were not even credited for their roles.

Trying to document these appearances is rather difficult, with the primary hindrance being the unavailability for viewing of several programs—some not seen since their initial network airing. There are, no doubt—and despite literally decades of research—appearances that have slipped through the cracks. While trying to be as thorough as possible, the following summary is limited to primarily U.S. rock and roll groups. For simplicity, a "group" is defined as three or more instrument-playing members, which leads to the exclusion of numerous appearances by duos such as the Righteous Brothers and Sonny & Cher or solo acts like Neil Diamond and Glen Campbell. Also excluded are musical groups in other non-rock and roll genres, such as the bluegrass Dillards' performances as the Darlings on six episodes of *The Andy Griffith Show,* the legendary Motown group the Supremes on *Tarzan,* tough girl group the Shangri-Las on *I've Got a Secret,* the great soul group the Five Stairsteps on *To Tell the Truth,* or the loungy Vagabonds' two appearances on *The Lucy Show.* The line is rather gray, however, so there might be some groups listed that err on the side of inclusion rather than exclusion. As a rule of thumb, however, if a scripted American prime time television program featured an appearance by a rock and roll group, it'll be included here within.

1964

The first known appearance by a rock group on a scripted U.S. television series occurred two months after the Beatles' first appearance on Sullivan's program. Obviously influenced by that appearance, Joey Bishop, on the "Joey, Jack Jones, and Genie" (April 11) episode of his *The Joey Bishop Show*, donned faux Beatles hair. In addition, the five-man band the **Crocodiles** were billed as "Joey's Grasshopper Band", yet they were referred to as simply the Grasshoppers. The story involved Joey dreaming that he's a rock star on *The Tonight Show* with guest star Ed McMahon making an appearance to introduce him and the **Crocodiles**. The band (drums, two trumpets, and two guitars) first played an instrumental, and then (switching to three guitars, drums, and sax) backed Joey for a number. Jack Jones also crooned two tunes.

Joey Bishop, replete with Beatles mop top, welcomed the Crocodiles on *The Joey Bishop Show* (1964). Photo from the author's collection.

The following month, on the March 24 "The Ladybugs" episode of *Petticoat Junction*, the Bradley daughters (Billy, Bobbie, and Betty

Joe Bradley along with friend Sally Ragsdale) formed their own Beatles' tribute band, the **Ladybugs**. Although the fictional group was created specifically for this series, they parlayed their roles by appearing on *The Ed Sullivan Show* two days prior—hence their inclusion here. Jeanne Riley, Pat Woodell, Linda Kaye Henning, and Sheila James performed the Beatles' 'I Saw Her Standing There' (changing "her" to "him") all the while wearing their influence on their sleeves. Incredibly, an article detailing the **Ladybugs** story stated, "the Beatles craze isn't over yet"—when it was barely even a month old!

THE ROCKLAND COUNTY JOURNAL-NEWS   NYACK, N. Y., TUESDAY, MARCH 24, 1964

T. V. Keynotes

'Petticoat Junction' Scores Beat With 'The Ladybugs'

By CHARLES WITBECK

The Lyons Den

When Screvane Stooped
They Took The Picture

The Ladybugs, one of the first Beatles-imitator groups, received top publicity. *The Rockland County Journal News* (March 26, 1964) detailed the group's formation. Article from the author's collection.

The only other documented appearance for 1964 was on an episode of the short-lived (13 episodes) Harry Guardino series, *The Reporter*. According to an interview with Brute Force by Chaim O'Brien-Blumenthal for *Ugly Things* 52, the **Tokens** appeared. The group had achieved several hits by the time of their appearance, with 'The Lion Sleeps Tonight' reaching #1 in 1961 (it was reissued on

RCA-Victor 447-0702 in 1964). Force (nee Stephen Friedland) had joined Hank Medress, Jay Siegel, Mitchell Margo and Philip Margo as songwriter and keyboardist for the **Tokens** not too long before this appearance. In the interview, Force didn't provide an episode titled but recalled that Elizabeth Allen guest starred, thereby identifying it as "The Lost Lady Blues", which aired on December 11. Force has never seen the episode and it's currently unavailable for viewing; as a result, the song(s) the group performed is unknown.

1965

There are assuredly other yet-to-be discovered appearance for 1964, but 1965 is much better documented. Shortly after the New Year, on January 6, the **Enemys** (Cory Wells, later of Three Dog Night, vocals; Mike Lustan, guitar; Dave Treiger, drums; and Cal Titus, bass) along with Annette Funicello guest starring as a club go-go dancer in a cage (reportedly filmed inside the Whisky a Go Go), appeared on the "Who Killed the Strangler?" episode of the Gene Barry detective series *Burke's Law*. The **Enemys** backed Funicello's dancing by playing a long instrumental as she shimmied along. Unfortunately, the band is relegated mostly to backdrop status, and is clearly seen only for a few, brief seconds. The quartet had very short hair compared to their cameo ten months later on *The Beverly Hillbillies*. After this appearance, in 1966, the **Enemys** released three 45-RPM singles on MGM Records. As a non-recording group prior to *Burke's Law*, their reputation as one of the hottest acts on the Sunset Strip no doubt led to their appearance.

Next, on the January 18 "Bugged by the Love Bugs" episode of *The Bing Crosby Show*, the **Standells** portrayed a band named the Love Bugs. They appeared throughout the episode performing various tunes, including "The Break Song", "Everybody Do the Ringo", "Someday You'll Cry", "Come Here" and, with Bing, "Kansas City". Larry Tamblyn recalled in his autobiography *From Squeaky Clean to Dirty Water* (BearManor Media, 2022), that, "The biggest thrill was when we backed up Bing Crosby singing 'Kansas City' . . . Surprisingly, Bing completely overcame his crooner image by really rocking the song. The show was a complete thrill for all of us." The **Standells** printed lineup for this appearance featured Larry Tamblyn, Gary McMillan (actually Lane), Emilio Bellissimo (aka Tony Valentino), and Joseph (in actuality, Dick) Dodd. The **Standells** were another hot California-based act that performed up and down the Sunset Strip and in San Francisco, where their *In Person at PJ's* album was recorded in 1964. In 1966, they recorded the garage punk classic 'Dirty Water'.

Crooning merged with Merseybeat on *The Bing Crosby Show* as the legendary actor/singer performed with the Standells. Larry Tamblyn and Gary Lane are seen behind Bing. Photo from the author's collection.

Although an animated sitcom, *The Flintstones* was broadcast in prime time before its syndication as a timeless afternoon children's cartoon favorite. Based during "modern stone age times" (prehistoric mixed with modern events, tools, etc.), on March 12, three guitarists were seen backing Jimmy Darrock (Darren) in the "Surfin' Fred" episode. The "band" is not credited nor mentioned by name, but Darren sings two tunes, "Surfin' Craze" and "Wax up Your Board", made popular by the **Fantastic Baggys** and released on their *Tell 'Em I'm Surfing* (Imperial 12270, 1964) album, leading to some online speculation that the group in question were the Baggys. The **Fantastic Baggys** were the popular '60's song writing duo of P.F. Sloan and Steve Barri, yet the group backing Darren is a three-man group (and, along with Darren, all play guitars!). As a result, it's a bit of a stretch to claim this as an appearance by the **Fantastic Baggys**.

Nearly a week later, on March 18, Eddie Munster proclaimed, "Hey Pop, those neat guys are the **Standells!**" who were making their second cameo appearance, this time on *The Munsters*. In the episode titled "Far Out Munsters", the **Standells** performed 'I Want to Hold Your Hand' and an original written by Pat and Lolly Vegas, 'Come On and Ringo' in the Munsters' living room. They appeared as themselves in this episode and were allowed some dialogue. In addition to their performance, Eddie played a **Standells** album on the living room turntable, Fred Gwynne as Herman reciting beatnik poetry, and Yvonne DeCarlo, as Lily, performed 'He's Gone Away.'

Al Lewis as Grandpa Munster bangs the drums in front of the Standells: Larry Tamblyn, Tony Valentino, Dick Dodd, and Gary Lane. Photo used with permission from Larry Tamblyn.

Less than two weeks later—you guessed it—the **Standells** were back on a prime time show. On March 29, on the "Three 'Lil Lambs" episode of medical drama *Ben Casey*, the band appeared in a night-club setting at The Place and performed an instrumental number. In a 2003 interview with author James Stafford, the **Standells'** Larry Tamblyn recalled, "It's interesting that…most of these shows were done in 1965, before the **Standells** ever had a hit record. Our co-manager had lots of ties to the movie industry. (Drummer) Dick Dodd was an original Mousketeer and I was from a showbiz family: actor Russ Tamblyn from *West Side Story* is my brother . . . plus, I had some acting experience. At the time that many of these shows were produced the Beatles were hot, and the media was looking for a good-looking rock group who could also act, to write into their stories. The **Standells** seem(ed) to fit the bill!"

The San Francisco Examiner (April 3, 1965) reported on Larry Tamblyn and the Standells' current appearances, including their cameo on *Ben Casey*. Photo from the author's collection.

The August 6, 1965, issue of *Rhythm & News* reported that "autograph hunters bogged down several tours when the **Missing Links** filmed a *McHale's Navy* segment at Universal City." How a 1960's rock group would be worked into a World War II Navy sitcom is unfortunately unknown (and it wouldn't be the last time this interesting plot point would be attempted). Based on the date of the paper, the only episodes that could have featured the band's appearance were in Season Four but review of the entire season failed to confirm the reported segment. To add to the confusion, it's also not known which "**Missing Links**" was being referred to. Although a local Los Angeles music paper, *Rhythm & News* covered the popular Australian band with that moniker, and there were at least three Los Angeles groups of the era utilizing the same name.

Here's the lone exception to the article requirement that all appearance be for prime time programs. Rock bands also appeared on daytime scripted television and, on September 27, Minnesota's **Castaways** (James Donna, keyboards; Robert Folschow, guitar; Roy Hensley, guitar; Dick Roby, bass; and Dennis Craswell, drums) riding the popularity of their hit song 'Liar Liar' (Soma 1433, June 1965), appeared on the debut episode of the teen soap opera *Never Too Young*. The show revolved around the popular teen club Alfy's High Dive and was produced by Joe Landis, who also was producer-director for the Los Angeles music show *Ninth Street West*. As a result, many hot groups that recorded hit songs in or around 1965 appeared. Over the course of 197 episodes, acts including the **Lovin' Spoonful** (December 16), the **Knickerbockers**, the **Sunrays, Bob Kuban & the In-Men, Mel Carter, Lou Rawls**, the **Ramsey Lewis Trio, Neil Diamond, Simon & Garfunkel, Marvin Gaye, Stevie Wonder, Johnny Rivers**, the **Yardbirds, Danny Hutton**, the **Beau Brummels** (October 28), **Paul Revere and the Raiders**, the **Girls**, and the **Gentrys** also appeared. Undoubtedly there were more. In his book *Liar Liar: The Story of Minnesota's Castaways in the 1960's* (Castaway Publications, 2002), Donna recalled their appearance as "the usual lip-syncing . . . as the crowd danced, while some talked at the tables. Fender amplifiers and a microphone on the stage made it look real, but nothing was plugged in as usual. Bob and Roy shared a mic, as was often done in those days. It was a lot of fun . . ."

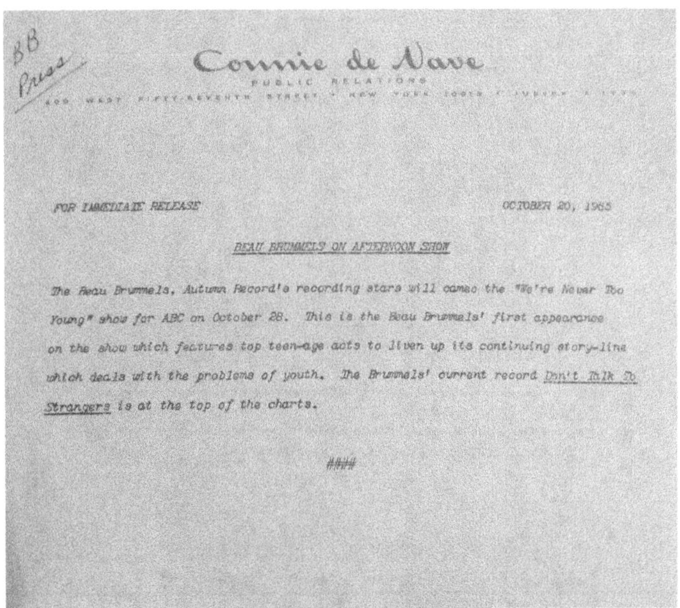

Press release announcing the Beau Brummels' appearance on *Never Too Young*. From the author's collection.

Two nights later—and back again to prime time—on September 29, the **Shindogs** appeared on the "Partying Is Such Sweet Sorrow" episode of *The Patty Duke Show*. The **Shindogs** (James Burton, Delaney Bramlett, Glen D. Hardin, Chuck Blackwell, and Joey Cooper) were at the time the house band for the *Shindig* television show and performed 'Hard Rock' and 'Rock On'. James Burton was also performing in Ricky Nelson's band on *The Adventures of Ozzie & Harriet*. Patty Duke herself chipped in by singing 'I'm Henry VIII I Am' (a song made popular by Herman's Hermits) and 'Funny Little Butterflies'. The first Shindogs single, 'Someday, Someday' b/w 'Why' (Warner Brothers 5665), was issued the following month.

Various newspapers around the country highlighted the Shindogs appearance on *The Patty Duke Show*. Articles from the author's collection.

On November 16, on *My Mother the Car*, in an episode titled "My Son, The Ventriloquist", the **Spats** performed 'She Kissed Me Last Night' (ABC-Paramount 45-10600, October 1964) on the set of an outdoor party patio, with a go-go girl in a red miniskirt shuggin' and fruggin' alongside the band. Created by Allan Burns and Chris

Hayward—the same duo that created *The Munsters*—the sitcom revolved around David Crabtree's (as portrayed by Jerry Van Dyke) mother being reincarnated as an automobile. The Spats were hot on the heels of their *Cooking with the Spats* (ABC-Paramount ABCS-502) album and had appeared on *American Bandstand* the prior year. The band's lineup at the time included Bobby Dennis, Mike Sulsona, Richard, Ron and Bud Johnson, Chuck Showalter, and Myron Carpino (who did not appear). Bud Johnson, in an interview with Mike Stax in *Ugly Things* 27, recalled the group was filmed playing live. "They told us, 'Boys, go set up there on the stage, plug in over there and play.' They put this great big microphone up there, a studio soundstage kind of mic, and that picked up everything. I couldn't believe it because it (sounded) as good as the record."

The Tustin News promoted the Spats prior to their appearance at Foothill High School. Article from the author's collection.

Unlike their background appearance on *Burke's Law*, the **Enemys** were put to much better use during their appearance on the classic "fish out of water" Buddy Ebsen-starring sitcom *The Beverly Hillbillies*. On the November 24 "Hoe Down A-Go-Go" episode", the **Enemys** appeared at the Whisky a Go Go (they were prominently billed on the marquee but it's likely the performance was on a set) and at a square dance in the Clampetts' mansion. They performed 'Mojo Woman', 'Oh Pretty Woman' and 'Turkey in the Straw' but also had speaking roles. As an interesting aside, this episode referenced the Beatles ("the most popular group in the world"), Freddie & the Dreamers, the Animals, and the Byrds.

Louis Paul, Jr. of the **Guilloteens** (with Laddie Hutcherson and Joe Davis comprising the trio)—who recorded for Hanna Barbera Records—did voice over work for many episodes of *The Flintstones* and other Hanna Barbera cartoons and claimed that his band made an appearance once, referred to in Flintstones' lingo as the Guillostones. Viewing of the entire series unfortunately contradicts this. According to the August 6, 1965, issue of *Rhythm & News*, however, it was reported that "the **Guilloteens** will be drawn into *The Flintstones* this fall". It's very possible, then, plans were changed, or the footage was cut prior to broadcast.

This belief is supported by an article in the August 30th, 1965, edition of the *Memphis Press-Scimitar,* which reported, "Later in the season, *The Flintstones* will have a takeoff on the current rock and roll popularity in an episode called 'Shinrock'. The **Guilloteens** cut the soundtrack for all the groups being parodied." That episode did come to fruition. Now titled "Shinrock A-Go-Go" and aired December 3, the program featured a Stone Age version of *Shindig*. Singing their huge hit, 'Laugh Laugh' (Autumn 8, December 1964), the **Beau Brummels** (Declan Mulligan, Ron Elliott, Ron Meagher, Sal Valentino, and John Peterson), referred to as the Beau Brummelstones, appeared three times: on Wilma's television screen, in the background of a nightclub, and again as the focal point of the nightclub scene. Other (faux) groups appearing that Betty and Wilma watched at the beginning of the show were Oscar & the Orangutans and the Wipe Outs—perhaps featuring the **Guilloteens**' soundtrack? *Shindig* host Jimmy O'Neil (Jimmy O'Neilstone) also appeared. While the **Guilloteens** were relatively short lived, they did record several classic songs that are highly regarded, including 'I Don't Believe' (Hanna Barbera HBR-446) and 'For My Own' (Hanna Barbera HBR-451). The **Beau Brummels**, one of the first American bands to challenge the Beatles on the charts and the first group from San Francisco to have a national hit, would record throughout the decade, releasing several 45s and five albums. Two of those albums, *Triangle* and *Bradley's Barn*, helped to lay the groundwork for country rock.

Ballard Native To Be On TV Show Tonight

A boy who lived his e a r l y years in Ballard County, Lad Hutcherson, will be seen on ABC television's "Shindig" show tonight.

Hutcherson is a member of the "Guilloteens" singing group, whose career is on the rise since signing with the Hanna-Barbera television producers.

He is the son of Mr. and Mrs. Albert Hutcherson, formerly of Blandville and Wickliffe, now living in Memphis.

The Guilloteens have appeared on the ABC show "Where the Action Is" and have appearances set later this season for NBC's "Hullabaloo" and the CBS Danny Kaye and Ed Sullivan shows. They have made the sound track for the Flintstones episode entitled "Shinrock," to be seen later in the season on ABC.

Local boy makes good as Laddie Hutcherson and the Guilloteens record a soundtrack for *The Flintstones*. Article from the author's collection.

Having performed "The Ballad of Davy Crockett", the theme song to the 1950's adventure series, and for Disney's "The Wonderful World of Color" (along with other themes released on Disneyland Records), the **Wellingtons** (Ed Wade, George Patterson, and Kirby

Johnson) later performed the opening credit's theme song for the first season of *Gilligan's Island* (a group named The Eligibles would perform the duties for the second and third seasons). On December 9, billed as **Les Brown Jr. and the Wellingtons**, they appeared in the episode titled "Don't Bug the Mosquitoes" of the same sitcom, playing the hip group, the Mosquitoes (Bingo, Bango, Bongo, and Irving). During their stay on the island, they performed 'Don't Bug Me' and 'He's a Loser'. The stranded castaways (Gilligan, the Skipper, the Professor, and Mr. Howell, not the 'Liar Liar' group!) also formed their own band, the Gnats, and rocked the island, hoping to encourage the Mosquitoes to rescue them. Ginger, Mary Ann, and Mrs. Howell formed the Honey Bees, and performed 'I Need You'. Strange Trivia 1: It was reported in several outlets prior to the episode airing that Sam Riddle of *Ninth Street West* and *Hollywood A Go Go* had replaced the **Wellingtons**. Strange Trivia 2: Contemporaneous newspapers articles listed *The Bing Crosby Show* as a recent television appearance for the **Wellingtons**. If it did indeed happen, the specific episode title is unknown.

Wellingtons Head Lineup at Holiday

The Wellingtons, who are regulars on ABC's "Shindig," and whose voices can be heard weekly on television's "Gilligan's Island," are now singing in the top spot of the Theatre Lounge show at the Holiday Hotel, which also features the Four Amigos and Charles Gould's Satin Strings.

"I Believe," "Night Train," "Blues In The Night," "Basin Street," "Some Enchanted Evening," "Flowers on the Wall," "What Now My Love," and a number of tunes made popular by the Tiajuana Brass, are some of the selections that demonstrate the versatility of the Wellingtons. The trio not only possesses lively harmony, but also provides outstanding instrumentals on guitar, bass, flute and piano. A quartet of musicians — piano, bass, guitar and drums—give them even greater musical depth.

Ed Wade, George Patterson and Kirby Johnson met and formed their popular musical group while attending the University of Illinois. All were active with the glee club and the threesome was often called upon to do special numbers. Their talents soon became well known throughout the Chicago area, and they found themselves making appearances at civic gatherings, industrial shows and conventions. That was the start of a professional career that has since taken them to leading night spots from New York's American Hotel to the Cocoanut Grove in Los Angeles.

Besides their regular appearance on "Shindig," the Wellingtons have also made a number of showings on other leading television shows, including Johnny Carson's "Tonight," the "Hollywood Palace," the "Bing Crosby Show," and recently made their acting debut in the "Don't Bug the Mosquitos" episode of the top-rated "Gilligan's Island."

The Wellingtons will keep audiences applauding in the Lounge through June 22.

An article promoting the Wellingtons' appearance at the Holiday Hotel summarizes the groups' TV appearances. Article from the author's collection.

On the December 29 "Too Many Cooks" episode of *Gidget*, an unknown group performed a cool instrumental in a high school gym. The group received several close-up shots and looked the part of a real band; unfortunately, they received no billing. This particular episode of the Sally Field sitcom dealt with Gidget's misadventures in dealing with three dates.

Having filmed a never-aired pilot two years prior, the same fate awaited **Jan & Dean** in 1965 as another proposed television series never progressed beyond the pilot stage. *On The Run*, directed by William Asher, featured the surfing duo in *Hard Day's Night*-styled shenanigans. The duo performed some of their biggest hits on stage, including 'The Little Old Lady (from Pasadena)' (Liberty 55704) and 'Surf City' (Liberty 55580). According to the official Jan & Dean website, "the new Jan & Dean vehicle would follow the antics of Jan & Dean as they traveled to new concert destinations each week—a sort of *Route 66* takeoff." The duo performed with a complete band behind them, hence the inclusion here. They also appeared, without backing band, on the July 1 episode of *Celebrity Game*.

Sometime in 1965, *Way-Out*, a Bart Ross/Frank Danzig TV production pilot, was filmed. According to George Caldwell of the **W.C. Fields Memorial Electric String Band** (Patrick Burke, Richard Fortunato, Steve Lagana, and Robert Zinner), the band's manager Al Burton was one of the producers of *Way-Out*. "We were going to be the house band, but the series didn't sell. I believe Al sold the idea to Ed Friendly and it became *Laugh-In*." It's possible the group was still known as the **Bees** (George Caldwell, Peter Ferst, Ron Reynolds, Cary Slavin, Robert Zinner, and John York, a later member of the Byrds), their earlier moniker, at the time filming began. The **Bees** had two 45s on the Mirwood and Mira labels while the **W.C. Fields Memorial Electric String Band** also recorded two singles, on Mercury and Hanna Barbera Records (HBR). Members would comprise several Los Angeles recording bands, including the Vejtables, and later permutations ESB and Fields.

1966

Opus 1 (Brian Decker, lead guitar and vocals; Doug Decker, guitar and vocals; Pete Parker, keyboards and vocals; and [John] Chris Christensen, drums and vocals) was the band behind the classic garage band single 'Back Seat '38 Dodge' (Mustang 3017, April 1966). On March 13, they appeared on stage at Henry's Coop as a backing band for a singer on the "Case of the Avenging Angel" episode of the lawyer program *Perry Mason*. According to Christensen, "We had the distinction of being in the very last black and white episode. We were supposed to be ourselves, but when we showed up, they called us Gabe & His Angels, and we mimed to some real fruity movie-rock-and-roll version of 'The Jersey Bounce.' They made Doug and Brian stand close together and in front of me to hide the bass drum head that (read) '**Opus 1**.'"

**Opus 1 portrayed Gabe & His Angels on *Perry Mason* (1966).
Photo used with the permission of John Chris Christensen.**

Also in 1966, a pilot titled *Rambling Wreck from Discotheque* (aka *The Man in the Square Suit*) was filmed and aired April 22 but not picked up as a series. From Jack Chertok Productions, it starred Paul Dooley as an older square hired to produce a teen rock and roll show. Despite plenty of music and dancing, a rock group was not featured. It's included here as a "what might have been" had the show ever moved beyond the pilot stage.

Any summary about prime time rock and roll groups would not be complete without at least a mention of *The Monkees*. Premiering on September 12, the Don Kirshner rock n' roll sitcom took scripted musical television to new heights. It's somewhat hard to believe that—despite all the singles, albums, hits, TV appearances (including *33 1/3 Revolutions per Monkee*, airing April 14, 1969) and the feature film *Head (1968)*—the show only lasted fifty-nine episodes. Since the program was about a struggling rock group trying to become the next Beatles, the music—and an early form of music videos—was an unquestioned highlight. Micky Dolenz, Davy Jones, Michael Nesmith, and Peter Tork all had some prior musical experience before landing their role. The top session musicians—including Carol Kaye and other Wrecking Crew personnel—initially performed on their records, leading to backlash at the time that the **Monkees** weren't a real group. History has corrected that incorrect belief, and the music of the **Monkees** will likely never go out of style.

There is an unknown band appearance in "The Committee for the 25th" episode of *Run for Your Life*, which aired October 3. This particular episode of the Ben Gazzara drama was set in San Francisco and involved the primary guest star, Brooke Bundy, dancing (to a cover of 'Downtown') in a cage in a club. The band was dressed in tuxedos but appeared to be a teen rock group—as opposed to the lounge acts that typically appeared on this TV show. The group was only very briefly glimpsed in the background.

Paul Revere & the Raiders (Paul Revere, keyboards; Mark Lindsay, sax, and vocals; Mike "Smitty" Smith, drums; Jim "Harpo" Valley, guitar; and Phillip "Fang" Volk, bass) were one of the house bands for Dick Clark's afternoon music program *Where the Action Is*. They also scored several hit records, including "Just Like Me" (Columbia 43461), "Kicks" (Columbia 43556), and "Hungry" (Columbia 43678). As a result, the **Raiders** were all over the airwaves for a few years and appeared frequently during prime time. Their second cameo, after *Never Too Young*, was on Adam West's pop smash DC Comics superhero sitcom *Batman*. In the November 2 "Hizzoner the Penguin" episode, the **Raiders** performed 'Vote for Penguin' (sung to the tune of 'Yankee Doodle Dandy') and an instrumental playing behind a belly dancer and, shortly after, while playing alone. Lindsay, in an interview with Greg Prevost in *Outasite #4*, recalled, "I remember it was all sort of surreal. They had Burgess Meredith as 'The Penguin.' He was running for mayor, and we were at his rally. All of a sudden, this belly dancer comes out of nowhere! I had no idea what was happening with that! It was pretty interesting the first time on a sound stage. It was bizarre, but it was fun." He also remembered that West, "Was a nice guy, but basically, they were more interested in 'Let's get the rock n' roll band in, and out.' We really didn't get much of a chance to hang." As an aside, Joel Eisner in *The Official Batman Batbook* (Contemporary Books, 1986), erroneously stated that "Paul Revere and the Raiders' presence in this episode marked the first appearance of any rock group on a sitcom," a "fact" that has been often repeated in the years after the book's publication. That, obviously, was incorrect.

Paul Revers & the Raiders on the sound stage for their *Batman* appearance. From the author's collection.

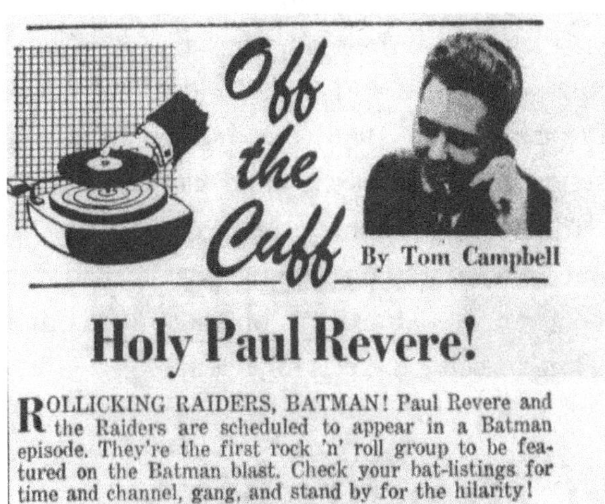

Holy Paul Revere!

ROLLICKING RAIDERS, BATMAN! Paul Revere and the Raiders are scheduled to appear in a Batman episode. They're the first rock 'n' roll group to be featured on the Batman blast. Check your bat-listings for time and channel, gang, and stand by for the hilarity!

Columnist Tom Campbell announced Paul Revere & the Raiders appearance on *Batman*. Article from the author's collection.

Approximately two weeks later, on the November 14 "A Slight Case of Music" episode of the short-lived *Jean Arthur Show*, the **Hubcaps** (Mike Dilley, Jim Dotson, and John Dotson) appeared. Unfortunately, this episode is unavailable for viewing but online summaries recap the plot as, "Lawyer Patricia Marshall gets into the rock 'n' roll music business when she helps her chauffeur's girlfriend sell a song." A group named the **Hubcaps** issued a single on Laurie Records (3219) but it's unknown if this was that same band.

Don Grady, who played Robbie Douglas on *My Three Sons*, was a musician before an actor and an actual member of the pop group the Yellow Balloon. He was also briefly involved with the Palace Guard and released a single with that band (Orange Empire 9164). Not surprisingly, Grady's musical abilities were showcased on the Fred MacMurray-starring sitcom, where his band the **Greefs** were seen rehearsing in the Douglas' living room and playing in a teen club. They also backed Jaye P. Morgan for a number, 'Gonna Get-cha', which was written by Grady. The episode in question, "Falling Star", aired on December 15. Grady recalled, "The **Greefs** were a real band, and we played many venues, bars, clubs, The Palladium in town. We never went on the road. They also recorded 'Good Man to Have Around the House' and 'The Children of St. Monica' (Canterbury C-501, November 1966) but by the time we hit the road with those songs the name of the band had been changed to The WindupWatchBand. I called them the **Greefs** because they were all my close friends. One of them could hardly play and was constantly asking me what the next chord was on stage! I eventually changed out the band but was able to keep my friends."

Grady's Greefs Features

As *My Three Sons* star Don Grady's real-life group, the Greefs received plenty of news coverage. This syndicated photo was printed in countless newspapers in 1966. Article from the author's collection.

Davie Allan and the Arrows were a popular Los Angeles group that scored a local hit record, 'Apache '65' (Sidewalk 1, 1964) in Southern California. They later frequently worked with Mike Curb to record several soundtracks to biker and exploitation flicks toward the end of the decade. In the first of two cameo appearances, the **Arrows** appeared on Don Adams' classic spy spoof *Get Smart*. In the "Kiss of Death" episode, aired on December 31, **Davie Allan** and two **Arrows** (Drew Bennett and Ross Viot) appeared uncredited playing at a KAOS party. They were seen in a handful of shots in one party scene. Although mostly relegated to the background, Allan recalled, "We were a bit surprised to hardly ever see Don. If he was in a scene, he would come to the set and someone would read him his lines and he would then repeat them for the camera. Hmmm . . . ."

The Sheriff, according to **Rising Sons** member Gary Marker, "Was a TV pilot film (but probably later whittled down to a one-hour pilot) produced by 20th Century Fox starring the has-been silent film star and now late Gilbert Roland. It wasn't a Western; it was a contemporary drama wherein Roland played the aged, soon to be retired, Sheriff of some fictional sparsely populated coastal county in Central California where hippies, surfers, bikers, and wealthy landowners all tended to congregate. The director was named Robert Gist who, by some accounts was once a pretty damn good actor/director with solid credentials. One of the extras in the beach scenes (the **Rising Sons** were the resident nighttime and day-time rock band, just hanging around this fictional county waiting for a chance to perform anywhere, apparently) was a funny, nervous little dark-haired guy name 'Dusty'. Ry Cooder befriended him and asked why whenever the cameras started rolling, he would put on dark glasses and fade to the back of the crowd. This was quite contrary to the usual deal where extras usually jostled and mugged for the camera, whenever possible. The guy explained, 'I plan on being a star someday and I don't want my face popping up later as just a chump-change extra.' If you haven't guessed already, it was

Dustin Hoffman. The **Rising Sons** contributed three songs to the film and several minutes of 'incidental music' and 'cues.' And we also did some acting if you call hanging around in the obligatory crowd scenes as 'hippie color' and delivering a few lines here and there acting. Our big-featured spot was playing a nighttime beach party scene, featuring two songs. We did a version of 'Statesboro Blues'…and an original called 'Sugar Pie', which was really a pastiche of traditional delta blues licks and purloined traditional lyrics that Taj Mahal altered a bit here and there, usually by supplying a different third line. Finally, we did a long, improvised acoustic 'cue' for a scene—a mournful slow drag blues with no lyrics and lots of harmonica." In addition to Marker on bass, Cooder on guitar and vocals, and Taj Mahal on vocals, harmonica, keyboards, and guitar, the **Rising Sons** included drummer Kevin Kelley and guitarist/vocalist Jesse Lee Kincaid.

1967

The January 31 episode of the spy series *The Girl from U.N.C.L.E.*, titled "The Drublegratz Affair", featured guest star Vito Scotti as "Dr. Igor Gork, who (developed) a death dealing 'multiple resonance detonator' which makes atoms dance to music. To concoct the correct musical chord—and bring a mountain down upon the head of the heir-apparent to the Tyrolean throne—Gork (employed) a rock 'n' roll group, portrayed by the **Daily Flash** Group". From Seattle, the **Daily Flash** (Don MacAllister, Doug Hastings, Jon Keliehor, and Steve Lalor) performed 'My Bulgarian Baby' (a song written specifically for the show with music by Gerald Fried and lyrics by Boris Sobelman), some instrumentals, and appeared in multiple scenes with some speaking roles. They released two singles on the Parrot and UNI labels. On *The Girl from U.N.C.L.E.*, stars Stephanie Powers danced to their music, while Noel Harrison posed for several photographs with the group.

Jon Keliehor, Doug Hastings, Noel Harrison, Steve Lalor, and Don MacAllister pose on the set of *The Girl from U.N.C.L.E.* Photo used with the permission of Bruno Ceriotti.

Although various sources, including *TV Guide* and contemporaneous newspaper listings, listed the band as The Factory Rock Quartet, actual credits for the February 9 "That's Showbiz" episode of the 1860's Wild West sitcom *F Troop* billed the combo as "**The Factory**". They appeared throughout as "The Bed Bugs," playing various instrumental tunes, including 'Camptown Races'. All songs were obviously being synched to. The group (pre-Little Feat Lowell George and Richie Hayward, Martin Kibbee, and Warren Klein) were also granted small speaking parts. The *F Troop* cast later formed a group, the Termites ("We eat our way into your hearts"), with Melody Patterson (Wrangler Jane) singing 'Lemon Tree' and' Mr. Tambourine Man', a song that wouldn't be written until one hundred or so years after the time frame this episode was set!

Don Grady's **Greefs** returned to *My Three Sons* in the "Now, In My Day" episode, aired March 2, and again performed 'Good Man to Have Around the House'. In this episode, "a class dance (led) to a romantic crisis for Chip, and Don Grady's (Robbie) Rock 'n' Roll group, the **Greefs**, appear(ed) as the school band." Grady recalled the members of the **Greefs** as Don Reigers on lead guitar, Wiley Rinaldi on rhythm guitar and Steve Tucker on drums, and informed that one-time Mousketeer Cubby O'Brien also drummed for the group. Contemporaneous articles identified the **Greefs** as Gil Rogers, Steve Tucker, Don Grady, and Wiley Rinaldi.

Teen-Age Letter Writers

Don Grady of My Three Sons knows where to find the top or pop artists of tomorrow.

"Just look at teen-age fan mail," he says. "Those girls don't just write letters. They turn out real works of modern art."

Grady made his discovery as a by-product of organizing his own combo, "Don Grady's Greefs," during a My Three Sons production hiatus. The series is broadcast Thursdays, 8:30 PM, on CBS.

"Don Grady's Greefs" rock 'n' roll combo, organized by Don Grady (right) of My Three Sons

The Greefs have been appearing in soda-fountain "night clubs" in Hollywood. They found themselves with a loyal band of fans after their opening night.

"The girls started writing us letters, but not just ordinary letters," Grady reports. "They use everything from nail polish to crayon stencils, in as many as 10 different colors. They do sketches of us and of themselves, decorative designs, symbolic drawings, hearts and flowers."

Rather than being done on canvas, the Greefs' budding pop and op art works come in on lined school tablets, graph paper, typing paper and fancy stationery in floral prints and pastel colors.

"Sometimes the girls make us feel guilty about spending their time on our mail rather than their homework," Grady says. "They'll do an especially fancy letter and write, 'Study hour is over soon so have to go.'"

One girl, apparently eager to make the Greefs think they had more fans than they actually did, disguised her handwriting and signed her name variously Cyndi, Cindi, Cindy, Cynthea and Cynthya.

"I think she ran out of changes, though," Grady says. "Lately she's just been writing to us as plain Cynthia."

Ego-shattering frankness is a characteristic of some of the mail, Grady reports.

"We got a letter from a girl written on pink paper in red, orange, blue and black ink that ended, 'Have to go now,' and explained that she was going to watch a competing television show."

More newspaper coverage for the Greefs' appearance on *My Three Sons*. Article from the author's collection.

An unsold 1966 CBS pilot titled *The Happeners*, directed by David Greene and written by Ernest Kinoy, aired on WPIX in New York on March 17. Cast members included Craig Smith and Chris Ducey (both would later join the Penny Arkade), Suzannah Jordan, Louis Gossett, and Louis Jacobi. A Plautus Production, the synopsis from an online footage house reads, "In the style of the Beatles' movies directed by Richard Lester, the story revolves around three young, hip folk-rock youth in Greenwich Village." *Ugly Things'* Mike Stax informed that, "The plot revolved around a struggling folk rock trio, the **Happeners**, based in Greenwich Village. The group was comprised of Craig Smith, Chris Ducey and Suzannah Jordan. According to Chris, the show (filmed in early/mid '66) was like a grittier, more real-life version of *The Monkees* (which it predated), shot kind of cinéma vérité style. The pilot apparently aired once but the show was never picked up. The Dave Clark Five performed on the pilot and acted. Chris remember(ed) Mike Smith had a scene interacting with the **Happeners** group. When the show didn't materialize, Smith and Ducey formed a duo, Chris & Craig, and recorded the great single 'Isha' for Capitol Records in the summer of '66. By '67 they had evolved into the Penny Arkade, and Mike Nesmith was acting as their producer. They recorded enough tracks for an album, but despite the high quality of the music nothing was ever officially released. The group broke up in early 1968. Some Penny Arkade tracks did surface though on the mega-rare LPs *Apache* and *Inca* self-released by Craig Smith circa '71 and credited to Maitreya Kali." Bob Bowers, who composed the music for *The Happeners*, recalled that, "We auditioned over 500 kids from New York City to Los Angeles and spent weeks in rehearsal and filming." In addition, the February 1966 issue of *Teen* reported that, while "auditioning R&Rs for a TV pilot, *The Happeners*, producer Buzz Berger listened with his mouth wide open to one group sing a ditty titled 'I've Got a Fungus Up My Nose from Fruggin' Through the Snows.'" Apparently, that band didn't pass, which sounds like a complete wasted opportunity!

Davie Allan & the Arrows made their second cameo appearance on Larry Cohen's science fiction series *The Invaders*. Starring Roy Thinnes as David Vincent, the premise of the show involved Vincent's learning of an alien invasion. While appearing as humans, the aliens could be identified by a deformed fourth finger. In "The Ivy Curtain", aired March 21, the group—like in their *Get Smart* appearance—performed an instrumental. **Davie Allan** and two **Arrows** (again Drew Bennett and Ross Viot) performed on stage in a school recreation room. The scene opened by focusing on the lead guitarist Allan, and then panned to highlight the entire group. According to Allan, the band, playing alien musicians, "pick-synched to an awful, pre-recorded track . . . (It) was cool because our opening scene showed my right hand like some of the aliens with the pinky finger sticking out. Jack Warden laughed at us because of our hair. How (did) we get involved? I love this one. We had recorded *The Invaders* theme. It was to be included on our *Cycle-Delic Sounds* . . . album. If you know anything about our producer, this might not be shocking: He took publishing (credit for the song) and changed the title to "Invasion". He also put my name as the writer, which could've saved his you-know-what if he'd been caught."

Making the second of their two cameo appearances, the **Factory** appeared on Jim Nabors' *Andy Griffith Show*-spinoff *Gomer Pyle, U.S.M.C.* on March 22. The "Lost, The Colonel's Daughter" episode featured the group performing two unreleased at that time songs: 'Lost' and 'Candy Cane Madness'. The group appeared very briefly on stage in a dark nightclub for two different scenes, but their performance was, for the most part, lost in the background during dialogue.

Later that month, trade ads announced, "Be prepared!" for **Every Mother's Son** TV debut on *The Man from U.N.C.L.E.* on March 31. The spy series had spun off *The Girl from U.N.C.L.E.* but was a few months late in welcoming a rock group cameo. In "The Five Daughters Affair" Part I", New York group **Every**

Mother's Son (Bruce J. Milner, Christopher Augustine, Dennis Larden, Larry Larden, and Schuyler Larsen) performed their hit song 'Come on Down to My Boat, Baby' (MGM K 13733, April 1967) while a major fight broke out in a nightclub. This show was concluded in two-parts; both parts were combined for a two-hour worldwide theatrical release titled *The Karate Killers*. The groups' affiliation on MGM Records no doubt had a part in their casting—*The Man from U.N.C.L.E.* was part of MGM Television. In an interview with Ted Liebler, Augustine recalled the cameo as the band's "biggest moment" (although they didn't receive billing). He added, "Appearing on *The Man from U.N.C.L.E.* exposed us to a national audience and gave us to in-roads to the West."

The July 29 issue of *Billboard* reported that, "TV and movies will play an increasingly important part in the activities of Screen Gems-Columbia Music and its sister company Col-Gem Records." The article stated the first major push would involve Sally Field and her starring role on *The Flying Nun*, with a Colgems single in the works for Field (at least four would be released on Colgems in 1967–68) and, eventually, and album on RCA Victor (*Sally Field: Star of The Flying Nun*, RCA Victor COM-106), which manufactured and distributed Colgems product. Lester Sill, who oversaw Colgems at the time, was quoted stating that he planned to have other Colgems artists "worked into" *The Flying Nun* scripts so they could get national TV exposure. In addition, the article continued that, "Another new TV series in which the publishing firm and the record division (would) be involved (was) *The Second Hundred Years* . . . On this show, too, Sill (planned) to work in his Colgems artists for that important TV exposure." The Monte Markham-starring series has largely been unavailable for viewing since its initial airing, however, and no Colgems artists are known to have appeared during the sitcom's twenty-six episode run. If one/some had, one possible episode could be the December 13 "Let My People Go Go", which involved, naturally, a go-go dancer.

The Weekend was an unsold pilot directed by Rod Amateau for United Artists that starred Tim Matheson, Tony Dow, Rick Kellman and Lorie Martin. The plot involved "the adventures of a group of high school teenagers who flock to the beach in Southern California each weekend for two days of fun in the sun." Apparently this one and only episode revolved around one of the characters trying to recover his repossessed motorcycle and no doubt lunacy ensued. While not picked to series, the "Like the Red Sea, Baby, We'll Never Part" pilot episode aired on September 9 and featured an appearance by the **Spats** (by now, Bobby Dennis, Mike Sulsona, Richard, Ron and Bud Johnson, Chuck Showalter, and Gregg DeLorto, an early member of Limey & the Yanks) in their second prime time cameo appearance. Mike Sulsona recalled that the pilot was "Filmed at Beverly Hills High School. We were a band that was playing for a dance in the gym and the stage parted over a swimming pool and all fell in." The group also recorded a song titled 'Weekend' with the intent of it being used as the show's theme song, but a different song with the same title was chosen instead. The **Spats'** version was never released.

On September 25, the **Strawberry Alarm Clock** appeared on *The Danny Thomas Hour*. According to *TV Guide*, in "The Scene", a dramatic episode, "Geraldine Chaplin (made) her American TV debut in this drama about a would-be painter's encounter with the hippie world. The **Strawberry Alarm Clock** appear(ed) in a psychedelic 'freak out' sequence." Along with Chaplin, Michael J. Pollard, Victor Buono, and Robert Stack appeared in the episode directed by Jack Arnold. The episode was originally titled "The Trip" but changed due to its drug content. The connotation likely led to the inclusion of the **Strawberry Alarm Clock,** best known for the very freaky (and catchy) 'Incense and Peppermints' (first issued as All American 373 and then released nationally as UNI 55018). This appearance is unfortunately not available for viewing.

The October 14 issue of *Billboard* reported that the Canadian group **Mandala** (four singles released across 1967 and 1968) had been signed to "include appearances in the new NBC-TV series *Ironside*", the Raymond Burr cop-in-a-wheelchair drama. This likely never happened as no appearances have yet come to light.

While Boyce & Hart might seem to fall outside the three-member band criteria established for inclusion, on the October 17 "Jeannie the Hip Hippie" episode of Barbara Eden's and Larry Hagman's fantasy sitcom *I Dream of Jeannie* they received billing as the **Tommy Boyce and Bobby Hart Band**. They appeared throughout the episode, and performed on multiple occasions, including in Major Nelson's living room, and in his car! Featured songs were 'Out and About' (A&M Records 858, June 1967) and 'Girl I'm Out to Get You'. Phil Spector also appeared. As a result of their work with the Monkees and, of course, their own hits, Boyce & Hart were in huge demand in the 1960s, which is in evidence by their cameo appearances. After *I Dream of Jeannie*, the duo appeared on *Bewitched* ("Serena Stops the Show", February 19, 1970) performing 'I'm Gonna Blow You a Kiss in the Wind' (Aquarian 380, September 1969) at the Cosmos Club; at one point, Serena played a Boyce & Hart album, and their hit 'I Wonder What She's Doing Tonight' (A&M Memories 75021 8577 7) was heard. The following month, on March 20, they appeared on *The Flying Nun* ("When Generations Gap") performing 'I Thank You' and 'Lonesome All the Time'. They were also reportedly slated to film a pilot titled *See How They Run* but it's not known whether it progressed beyond the developmental stage.

Boyce and Hart Get Unique 3-way Pact

The multi-talented team of Tommy Boyce and Bobby Hart has concluded an unprecedented multi-million dollar contractual agreement with three companies within the Columbia Pictures Industries, Inc., organization: Screen Gems, Bell Records and Screen Gems-Columbia Music, Inc., for television, recordings and music publishing, respectively.

The announcements were made today by Jerome S. Hyams, executive vice president of Columbia Pictures Industries, Inc. and president of the Screen Gems division.

Specifically, the agreements call for (A) Screen Gems to develop and produce a network television series starring Boyce and Hart, (B) the creation of Boyce and Hart's Aquarian Records, a new label that will be distributed worldwide by Bell Records, and (C) the renewal of the long-term music publishing contract with Screen Gems-Columbia Music which had been in effect since 1964.

Hyams said: "Screen Gems' preeminent position in these three areas of the entertainment field will enable Boyce and Hart to realize the maximum potential from their creative efforts."

Leonard Goldberg, vice president in charge of television production for Screen Gems, will supervise the development of the new Boyce and Hart television series; Larry Uttal, president of Bell Records, will direct the distribution of Boyce and Hart's Aquarian Records; and Emil LaViola, vice president and general manager of Screen Gems-Columbia Music and Lester Sill, West Coast vice president of the company, will continue to coordinate Boyce and Hart's music publishing activities.

In connection with the television series, Goldberg announced the opening of offices for Boyce and Hart's Aquarian Productions at the Screen Gems-Columbia Studios in Hollywood.

In the records area, Uttal said that the first Boyce and Hart single on their record label will be released the first week in August. In the five years that Boyce and Hart have been associated with Screen Gems-Columbia Music, they have written more than 260 compositions which have sold nearly 50 million records that have been recorded by many leading artists throughout the world.

The duo's most recent album, with their latest compositions, is titled "It's All Happening on the Inside."

Boyce and Hart also wrote, produced and recorded the song, "L.U.V.," which provided the focal point for a national campaign to peacefully lower the voting age to 18.

Among the many television programs on which the team has made appearances are "I Dream Of Jeannie," "Hollywood Palace," "The Steve Allen Show," "The Pat Boone Show" and "The Woody Woodbury Show" and regular appearances on "The Joey Bishop Show."

As top songwriters, including for the Monkees, Boyce & Hart were in high demand. Article from the author's collection.

On October 26, the **Pleasure Fair** (Tim Hallinan, lead and backing vocals; Michele Cochrane, lead and backing vocals; Robb Royer, backing vocals and guitar; and Stephen Cohn, backing vocals and guitar) appeared on the Raymond Burr drama *Ironside*. The Universal recording artists were seen performing their original song 'Turnaway' (the sheet music is prominently displayed before the group appeared; the song appeared on their self-titled *The Pleasure*

Fair LP, UNI 3009, October 1967) in the Mastercut Recording Studio in the "Tagged for Murder" episode.

The next night, the **Peppermint Trolley Co.** (Patrick McClure, guitar, and background vocals; Danny Faragher, keyboards, and background vocals; Casey Cunningham, drums; and Jimmy Faragher, bass, and lead vocals) made the first of their two cameo appearances in the October 27 "Robin Hood & the Sheriff" episode of *The Beverly Hillbillies*. The group performed outdoors at Los Angeles' Griffith Park, in the second half of a two-parter. Among the dancers to their music was Ellie Mae dressed in Robin Hood garb…and a monkey! Danny Faragher recalled on his website that, "We wore silly wigs supplied by the Paramount costume department, but it was fun! We were treated well."

The following night, on October 28, Joe *Mannix* tracked "a missing coed through a hippie dream world of hallucinogenic drugs, hard rock music and obscure poetry." Inhabiting that world were the **Buffalo Springfield**. The "Warning: Live Blueberries!" episode featured the group performing in two separate nightclub scenes at The Lost Dimension; while playing 'For What It's Worth' (Atco Records 45-6459, December 1966) and 'Bluebird' (Atco Records 45-6499, June 1967), their music was mostly drowned out by dialogue. 'For What It's Worth', with its "It's time we stop hey, what's that sound? Everyone look, what's going down?" lyrics, would become an anthem for the decade. According to a contemporaneous article, the "Springfields" were comprised of "Richard Furay, Doug Hastings, Stephen Stills, Fim Fielded and Dewey Martin". There must have been some time lapse between the filming of the **Buffalo Springfield** appearance and the article; "Fim Fielded" is presumed to be Jim Fiedler, a later member. Bruce Palmer and Neil Young were both visible in the *Mannix* episode. Interestingly, according to Stills when he recounted the *Mannix* appearance and his regret in not recording live performances in an interview with Andy Greene for *Rolling Stone*, "The best sound we ever got was when we did this stupid TV show where we played just a little bit of a song and we were like, 'Oh, my God, that's the sound we've been looking for . . . It was the only place we could get that sound right."

Brook Bundy guest starred along with Buffalo Springfield on *Mannix*. Ad from the author's collection.

Despite Johnny Green's claims in some online interviews that his group the **Greenmen** made multiple appearances on *Batman* they, in fact, only appeared in the November 16 episode titled "Surf's Up, Joker's Under". The **Greenmen** included Marilyn Campbell, Johnny Green, Richard Person, John Trombatote, and Robert Van Holten. The group, with green hair, was seen performing 'I Dream of Jeannie with the Light Brown Hair' and 'A Little Bit Harder' on a beach.

The Greenmen were a popular Midwest rock and show band that moved to Los Angeles. In Mark Starks' book, *Johnny Green & The Greenmen: The Incredible True Story of the Green-Haired Entertainer and His Top-Rated Show Band*, Green also reported his group made a brief and silent appearance on an episode of *Star Trek* where they slid down some "plastic tubes"; that the band's "green hippie wheels van", with **Johnny Green & The Greenmen** painted on the side, made a brief appearance in an episode of *The Mod Squad*; that his Reactor car was used in an episode of *Bewitched* and as Catwoman's (Ertha Kitt) ride in a different episode of *Batman*; that he submitted material to Greenway Productions for the band's hopeful appearance on *The Green Hornet* (the show was cancelled before the band could be considered); and that the group auditioned for *The Monkees*, as the Green Monkees—with green hair. As for the *Batman* appearance, upon seeing the Greenmen, Chief O'Hara, played by Stafford Repp, stated, "I've heard of long-haired musicians, but never green-haired ones. Maybe they've got some connection to the Joker?" Green recalled, "It (the *Batman* cameo appearance) was a big deal. We had our own private dressing room, our own star on the door. We went from not eating to eating tacos."

The Greenmen used their appearance on *Batman* to help promote their personal appearances. This ad was printed in Oshkosh, Wisconsin. Ad from the author's collection.

Another issue of *Billboard*, this one from November 25, reported that the **Lewis & Clarke Expedition** (Travis Lewis aka Michael Martin Murphey, vocals, guitar, harmonica; Boomer Clarke aka Owen Castleman, vocals, guitar; John London, guitar, bass; and Ken Bloom, guitar, keyboards) was slated to appear on an episode of NBC-TV's *Daniel Boone*. This news was also reported in newspapers and in *Go* magazine. Several reports outlined the plot ("the group will portray five youngsters who run a whisky [sic] still until they are jailed by the British and ultimately rescued by Daniel Boone"), the episode title, "Auld Lang Syne", and even the song they'd perform, 'Freedom Bird.' However, Boomer Castleman confirmed the group did not appear. They did, however, agree to "compose two songs for Ed Platt, who'll sing them in upcoming episode of TV's *Get Smart*." It's unknown if that ever occurred.

Of course he has been a regular visitor to most homes for the past four years on the television show "Daniel Boone."

Are you ready for this? The **Lewis and Clarke Expedition** has been signed to guest star on the "Auld Lang Syne" segment of the same show. The group will portray five youngsters who run a whisky still until they are jailed by the British and ultimately rescued by Daniel Boone.

The group will sing its **"Freedom Bird"** on the show which will be aired on NBC early in the spring.

Syndicated newspaper reports detailed the Lewis & Clarke Expeditions' cancelled appearance on *Daniel Boone*. Article from the author's collection.

The **Visions** (Billy O. Dalton, Chuck Morgan, Gary R. James, and Ray Sutton) released a handful of singles on the Vimco label in their native Texas in 1965 and 1966. After relocating to Hollywood, they appeared on *Run for Your Life* in the December 22 "Fly by Night" episode playing one of their post-Texas singles songs, 'Small Town Commotion' (UNI 55042, December 1967) on stage in a dark night-club/bar. Actor Don Stroud joined them on stage.

1968

It's been rumored that the **Sacred Cows** from the January 13 "Groovy Guru" episode of *Get Smart* were members of a real band named Beautiful Daze, who recorded the classic 'City Jungle'. **Sacred Cow** member John Greek, however, informed T. Mike of the Rocklopedia Fakebandica website that "the **Sacred Cows** were Jerry Scheff (bass), John Greek (guitar) and Ben Benay (guitar). Although a record by the Beautiful Daze that I played on and co-wrote was released just before this TV show, Scheff and Benay had nothing to do with the 45. We were all backup musicians on the road with the Fifth Dimension during the summer of '67, so we all knew each other. We were all doing 'session work' around L.A." The **Cows** appeared in this episode wearing fuzzy cow horn hats and sunglasses and played some wild fuzz riffs while Max and 99 tried to escape. The great Larry Storch played the Groovy Guru. Although not a true band per se the individual members were musicians and not actors, hence the inclusion.

Drummer Evan Zang recalled on Chris Bishop's Garage Hangover website that, "From 1967 and on, and with many thanks to a local deejay, Casey Kasem, who managed us, we were one of the very rare South Bay pop bands that graduated from playing high school dances to the more lucrative and prestigious Hollywood scene." Appearing in both episodes of a two-part crime drama *Felony Squad* ("The Flip Side of Fear", Part One aired on January 15 and Part Two on January 22) was Zang's band, whose drumhead read "**The Candy Company**". Although the group (Joey Campo, bass; Sam Chirico, rhythm guitar; Jim Whittle, lead guitar; and Even Zang, drums), had recorded unreleased songs using that moniker (and previously as the Royal Teens ['Tears in My Eyes' b/w 'Chicanery', Rev Records 45-115-67 in 1967]), they would release a single ('Butterfly High' and 'Sleepy Hollow People') in March on the VMC label (V 719, March 1968) under the name the **Paper Fortress**. Their brief appearance in Part One was limited to performing an instrumental in a recording studio. Part Two offered much more screen time as the group played (another instrumental) at a party where they received some quality screen time. Zang recalled, "We were on screen about four minutes but it took all day to film."

The debut show of the Rowan and Martin hosted hodgepodge of music and comedy, *Laugh-In*, aired January 22, featured a promo film of the **Strawberry Alarm Clock** performing 'Tomorrow'. Later shows featured similar promo films by the **Nitty Gritty Dirt Band** and the **First Edition** (January 29), while the **Monkees** appeared as non-musical guests and the **Holy Modal Rounders** performed 'You've Got the Right String, Baby, But the Wrong Yo-Yo'. The **Temptations,** the **Curtain Calls** (who performed the terrible vaudeville-ish *Laugh-In* cash-in 'Sock it to Me Sunshine' on April 15) and faux group the **Banana Splits** also appeared, while the January 20 issue of *Billboard* reported that the **Sunshine Company** had signed for an appearance; whether or not it happened is unconfirmed.

A real headscratcher, the **Sundowners** cameo on Robert Wagner's thief working for the U.S. government action series *It Takes a Thief* highlighted the group in several close-ups over the course of several minutes while they performed their song 'Dear Undecided' from their *Captain Nemo* LP (Decca DL 75036, 1969)—yet they received no billing and were referred to as "the Raspberry Wristwatch." Talk about a wasted opportunity for song promotion. In addition to their single, the band performed an instrumental at a swank party in the February 6 "A Very Warm Reception" episode. Dominick Demieri of the **Sundowners** recalled that this appearance was "the best TV shot we ever appeared on."

The Sundowners, portaying the Raspberry Wristwatch, pose on the set of *It Takes a Thief*. Photo from the author's collection.

Unlike the uncredited Sundowners, *Ironside* was a safe bet to either name drop a group or to bill them in the end credits. In one of the better rock group cameo appearances, the **Hook** (Bobby Arlin, guitar and vocals; Buddy Sklar, bass and vocals; and Craig Boyd, drums) appeared March 21 on *Ironside's* aptly-named "A Trip to Hashbury" episode. They appeared in two great scenes inside a hippie drug commune. Raymond Burr watched the second song from his ever-present wheelchair in a classic stoic stare. Two **Hook** songs, 'Son of Fantasy' and 'Plug Your Head In' (UNI 55057, March 1968), both also on their UNI Records' *The Hook Will Grab You* LP (UNI 73023, 1968), were featured for almost ten minutes in this episode (UNI Records was owned by Universal Studios, producer of *Ironside*). When Ironside showed up at commune, the **Hook** briefly performed a cool version of the *Ironside* theme song!

Another group to receive credit and ample screen time for their cameo appearance were the **Seeds** (Sky Saxon, Jan Savage, Rick Andridge, and Daryl Hooper). Although playing a band named the

Warts on the April 28 "How Not to Manage a Rock Group" episode of the sitcom *The Mothers-in-Law*, they performed their 1967 smash 'You're Pushin' Too Hard' (GNP Crescendo GNP 364X, November 1965) in a living room setting. To balance out the cool factor for the older target audience, they also played 'Some Enchanted Evening.' At the time of their appearance, the **Seeds** were considered pioneers of the entire "Flower Power" movement, and their colorful appearance capitalized on their popularity. 'You're Pushin' Too Hard' is still considered one of <u>the</u> great garage punk songs.

Darryl Hooper, Sky Saxon, Rick Andridge and Jan Savage, the Seeds, gape in awe over Eve Arden, Herbert Rudley, Kaye Ballard and Roger Carmel on the set of *The Mothers-In-Law*. Photo from the author's collection.

It was reported that "*Peyton Place* executive producer Paul Monash and producer Everett Chambers have singed the **Pillory**, a new A&M Records rock group for recurring roles in the 20th Century Fox Television series airing over on ABC-TV". Although their total number of appearances on the nighttime soap opera is undocumented (it's believed to be somewhere between five and ten), the **Pillory** made their debut on the June 27 (some reports stated June 24) "Tom Winter Convinces Jill to Stay" episode.

Dressed in matching orange outfits with Puritan collars, they performed Boyce & Hart's 'Teardrop City' (also recorded by the Monkees) and two unknown songs at the Shoreline, an underground hangout. Jeff Kramer, a recurring character on the show, played keyboards and, Nancy, a female guitarist, sang as the band's scene faded out. The blind pianist was named Chris Webber, portrayed by Gary Haynes. Suzannah Jordan portrayed Nancy and listed Kerim Capli (of Groop, Ltd. and the Sundowners), Wayne Erwin, Al Collini, and John Findlater as comprising the rest of the **Pillory**. (Reports at the time listed Lindy Getz on drums, Gregory Barton on bass guitar, Steve Pitts on rhythm guitar, Kerim Capli on lead guitar and Suzannah "Gordon" doubling on electric 12-string guitar and vocals.) As documented earlier, along with Craig Smith and Chris Ducey, Suzannah had earlier filmed a pilot for *The Happeners*. Suzannah wrote most of the songs that the **Pillory** performed on the show, and they were recorded at A&M Studios. Titles included 'Castles of Sand', 'Soul Canary', 'Weep with Me', 'Skinny Man', and 'Missing You' (also written by Boyce & Hart). According to Suzannah, the **Pillory** never performed live. She became a staff writer for A&M and the band all went their separate ways. As for her time on *Peyton Place*, Suzannah recalled that, "I enjoyed my time on the 20th Century Fox lot. They were writing lines for my character Nancy, so I was getting to act a bit as well as sing. We got to work with different directors, and we each got our own trailer to hang out in. I remember Barbara Parkins coming to see me one day asking me about singing. She said she wished she could sing. She was very nice and very beautiful. Ryan O'Neal was very hyperactive, and you sure knew when he was around. He was an extremely high-octane guy. Barbara Rush was so beautiful and had that star aura about her. I wish I had met Mia Farrow, too! I got to attend with John Findlater movie premiers and publicity functions arranged by the studio, which were a lot of fun. He was a really nice guy."

The cast of *Peyton Place*, including the Pillory, pose for *TV Guide*. Photo from the author's collection.

It should also be noted that the **Penny Arkade** (Don Glut and Bobby Donaho with Craig Smith and Chris Ducey from *The Happeners*) had initially auditioned for the role of the *Peyton Place* house band. According to bassist Glut, "We would have been recurring characters of sorts. The idea was that there was a nightclub that would be a continuing location in the series. We would have been the house band for that club . . . we went down to the Columbia Studios/Screen Gems lot . . . dressed in our blue suits . . . and played a couple songs. I think this took place on a soundstage but can't remember exactly. The people we auditioned for really seemed to like us and, cocky us, we pretty much thought we'd won the gig, also considering Mike Nesmith's association with Columbia/Screen Gems. I don't think there had been any other bands trying out for this, until . . . someone who was the son of one of the Screen Gems bigwigs literally threw a band together overnight, auditioned the next day with a couple cover songs—and got the gig. (I've) never heard of **Pillory** . . . or if I did, I've forgotten."

What Gap?, a half-hour pilot for a sitcom that wasn't picked up, was aired by ABC as a TV special on September 9, 1968. The show starred Wally Cox as "the Square", who tried to bridge the "generation gap" after meeting a girl in San Francisco. One of the ways he did so was by "grooving" to the **Chamaeleon Church**. Interestingly, on April 14, a TV special by the name of *Preview!* was aired. Hosted by Adam West, the show examined the "now" scene in music, fashion, movies, and athletics. Included were segments on The Group Image ('Open Your Heart'), Dionne Warwick, and the **Chamaeleon Church** ('Camillia Is Changing', from their self-titled album, MGM E4574, September 1968). Why is this interesting? According to **Chamaeleon Church** member Ted Myers, "We only made one TV appearance. That was . . . the show called *Preview!* on ABC, which aired on Easter Sunday." Myers had no recollection of *What Gap?* However, both programs were produced by David Yarnell. Is it possible that Yarnell took the **Chamaeleon Church** footage from *Preview!* and incorporated it into *What Gap?* As of now, this possibility is only a best guess.

The season premiere of Lucille Ball's sitcom *Here's Lucy* ("Mod, Mod Lucy", aired September 23) featured her son, Desi Arnaz, Jr., as Craig Carter drumming for his teen band. It's not known whether this group featured actual musicians or actors. Desi, of course, was a member of teen rock band Dino, Desi & Billy, along with Billy Hinsche and Dean Martin's son, Dean Paul Martin ("Dino").

On September 24, the cool/hippie cop drama *The Mod Squad* premiered. The "Teeth of the Barracuda" pilot episode of the popular show featured the **Other Half** (Randy Holden, Geoff Westen, Larry Brown, Ron Saurman and Jeff Nowlen). The band was seen performing their song 'Oz Lee Eaves Drop' (Acta 45-825, May 1968) in a nightclub, filmed at the Spectrum 2000 club (previously Ciro's). In an interview with Mike Stax in *Ugly Things* 48, Westen recalled, "We got that (the cameo) through my dad. He worked on the show . . . All I told my dad was, 'Make sure you get some shots of me!' I got about one second; that was it!" In fact, the entire band's footage was relatively brief, but the song was played in its entirety. Another **Other Half** song, 'Bad Day' (Acta 45-819, February 1968) was also heard in a nightclub scene, but the band was not seen performing it.

Also debuting September 24 was the premier episode of *That's Life*, "How We Met". This show is unavailable for viewing but, according to *TV Guide*, "Robert Morse and E.J. Peaker star in this weekly Broadway-paced blend of comedy, music and romance . . . The rocking **Turtles** perform in a discotheque sequence." The songs performed were 'Eleanor' (White Whale WW 276, September 1968) and 'Battle of the Bands' (from their *Present the Battle of the Bands* album, White Whale WWS-7118, 1968). The Turtles, of course, were best known for the timeless "ba ba ba" sing along song 'Happy Together' (White Whale WW 244, 1967) but scored several hits including 'It Ain't Me, Babe' (White Whale WW 222), 'She'd Rather Be With Me (White Whale WW 249) and a slowed down remake of the Byrds' 'You Showed Me (White Whale 292). The group's assumed line-up for this appearance included Howard Kaylan, Mark Volman, Al Nichol, Jim Pons, and Johnny Barbata.

A pre-airing article shares the details on *That's Life*, including the guest appearance by the Turtles. Article from the author's collection.

Two nights later, on September 26, the **Sundowners** made their second prime time appearance in the first show of the Sally Field's post-*Gidget* sitcom *The Flying Nun's* second season episode, "Song of Bertrille". The capsule description for *TV Guide* listed them as a "way-out rock group." The band was seen in a handful of scenes, the highlight being their performance at the Casino Carlos A Go Go, where they (with singer/actor Paul Petersen taking lead vocals) performed 'A Whole New World' on stage amidst flashing strobe lights while flanked on both sides by go-go girls dancing in cages. It's an incredibly cool and strange scene that one would be hard pressed to identify as being from *The Flying Nun* if not for the flashes of Sally Field in her habit interspersed throughout the performance. Sally also sang 'A Whole New World' on two different occasions, though her version paled in comparison to the **Sundowners'** take on the song, which featured the "psychedelic" phrases that the band added, such as "Turn On", "Higher Than High", "Magic Mushrooms", etc. According to the **Sundowners'** Bobby Dick, the role was originally intended for the Turtles; maybe they were busy filming their *That's Life* appearance? In addition to Bobby Dick, the **Sundowners** included George Bianchi, Dominic Demieri, Edmund Brick, Benny Grammatco and Edwin Placidi. In contrast to Demieri's belief that their *It Takes a Thief* performance was the **Sundowners'** best TV appearance, this one might actually top it.

SUNDOWNERS TO APPEAR—
The Sundowners, Decca recording stars, will make a special appearance Sunday from 2 to 6 at the Rialto Theatre. The group, which has appeared in such TV shows as the "Dick Clark Show," "The Flying Nun" and "To Catch a Thief," also appeared in the recent movie, "Don't Make Waves."

Although the Sundowners originated in the Glens Falls area, they have spent most of their time in Las Vegas, Hollywood and San Francisco. They also took part in the Monkee Concert Tour and have performed at the Hollywood Bowl and the Miami Auditorium.

"Beach Blanket Bingo" will be shown on the screen and a second group, The Karyn, will also perform.

The Sundowners consist of George Bianchi, Edmund Brick, Dominic Demieri, Robert Dick, Benny Grammatco and Edwin Placidi. They will also appear at the Village Inn, South Glens Falls, on Sunday night.

Both groups are under the management of Tom D'Angelo of Glens Falls.

Stenographer Test Scheduled

Mrs. Joyce R. Grey, executive secretary of the Warren County Civil Service Commission, has announced that the commission will hold an open-competitive examination for senior stenographer on March 1 to establish an eligible list. The salary for this position varies in each location. An applicant is required to take dictation at a rate of 90 words per minute to qualify. Applications may be picked up at the office of the commission at the Warren County Municipal Center or will be mailed upon request. Applications must be received no later than Jan. 29.

Newspaper articles for the Sundowners' appearance at the Rialto Theater recapped the band's numerous cameo appearances. Article from the author's collection.

The Sundowners received *TV Guide* billing for their appearance on the Sally Field sitcom, *The Flying Nun*. Ad from the author's collection.

In the nearly forgotten Carl Betz-starring legal drama *Judd for the Defense*, the **Pearly Gate** (Harold "Lucky" Floyd, Bobby Smith, Jimmy Marriot, and, unfortunately, two unidentified members), formed from the remnants of the great Texas garage band the Sparkles ('No Friend of Mine') opened the October 25 "Sound of the Plastic Axe" episode in what appeared to be a high-rise apartment building while playing behind a woman in a large, brass bed. The band wore matching orange jackets with large, black lapels and, tying to the episode's title, their name was The Plastic Axe! Newspapers reported, "Cast in the role of the Plastic Axe rock group are five young men who found that they worked so well together they could continue in the entertainment world as a unit."

PEARLY GATE is at Ron Stevens' Lemon Tree for a nine-day engagement. The group appeared on the television program "Judd for the Defense," only weeks ago.

Promotional pieces for the Pearly Gate touted their guest appearance on *Judd for the Defense*. Article from the author's collection.

The Name of the Game alternated stars Gene Barry, Robert Stack, and Anthony Franciosa in a drama about characters associated with Howard Publications. On November 1, the **Poor** (Randy Naylor, Randy Meisner, Pat Shanahan, and Allen Kemp), on the "Shine on, Shine on Jesse Gil" episode, made the first of their two cameo appearances on the program. They appeared performing an unknown song outdoors in a park but were largely obscured by dancing teens and children. The band was also very briefly seen during the opening credits, behind Darren McGavin's credit.

Six nights after their appearance on *The Name of the Game*, on November 7, the **Poor** appeared in a nightclub scene on *Ironside*. In an episode titled "Price Tag: Death", the group received several close-up shots and, although unbilled, their name was visible on the drum kit.

The Poor, Randy Naylor, Randy Meisner, Pat Shanahan, and Allen Kemp, on the set of *Ironside*. Photo from the author's collection.

Although a different lineup than the group that cameoed on *The Beverly Hillbillies* (this time the band included Danny Faragher, Jimmy Faragher, Casey Cunningham, and Greg Tornquist), the **Peppermint**

Trolley Co. (also listed as simply "Peppermint Trolley") appeared on *Mannix* on November 16. In "Who Will Dig the Graves?", Mike Connors, as Joe Mannix, walked in on the band while they were rehearsing their song 'Trust' (Acta 45-829, August 1968) in the California Recording Studio. Though a recording rehearsal, the band was completely decked out in their best '60's performance garb. In a *TV Guide* summary for the episode, it was reported that the group was "no match for Lalo Schifrin's marvelous music for the series"! Interesting aside: The **Peppermint Trolley Co.** was signed to perform the theme song for a new family comedy premiering in 1969—*The Brady Bunch*! **Trolley** member Danny Faragher recalled the band recorded the instrumental and multi-part vocals for the pilot, but their vocals were taken off and replaced for the series. The backing music is still them. (The **Peppermint Trolley Co.** version can still be heard on YouTube.) The group reportedly did, however, perform the theme for *Love American Style* for one year, as did the Cowsills.

Rock music group of RHS alums to play

A rock music group known as "Bones," comprised of four RHS alumni, will return to the campus Saturday night to play for a dance in Terrier Hall from 9-12 p.m.

With the assistance of the high school PTA, the senior class is sponsoring the dance at a cost per student of $1.50 without ASB card and $1.25 with card. Non-student guests will be permitted with courtesy cards only. The current school dress code will be in effect.

Lynn Chedester is the senior chairman for the dance and is being assisted by Cindy Donald and Liz Nielsen.

Providing music with an emphasis on hard rock, the "Bones" (formerly known as the Peppermint Trolley Comany), have recently made several recording sales.

The group has appeared in many cities across the United States and television shows including Boss City, the Donald O'Connor Show, Dick Clark, U-beat, and in the series Mannix and The Beverly Hillbillies.

Members are Danny Faragher on electric piano; Jimmy Faragher, bass and lead singer; Greg Tornquist on guitar; and Casy Cummingham on drums. Another Redlands alumnus, Steve Hauser, manages the group.

An article on Bones, a post-Peppermint Trolley Co., group name, lists the band's several cameo appearances. Article from the author's collection.

The December 5 "No Blue Skies" episode of Jack Lord's police procedural *Hawaii Five-O* featured an uncredited backing band that received a great deal of screen time. They weren't really a *rock* group, as they featured a xylophone and large bass . . . but they did perform 'Going Out of My Head' (along with 'This Land Is Your Land', 'It Only Takes a Moment' and 'I'll Remember You') while backing Joey Rand as played by Tommy Sands. Sands, a former singing teen star who made a splash playing a riff of Elvis Presley on the January 30, 1957 "The Singing Idol" episode of *Kraft Television Theater*, which begat the feature film *Sing Boy Sing* the following year, portrayed a nightclub singer who doubled as a cat burglar.

Completing their cameo trifecta—and all in 1968—on December 20 the **Poor** made their second appearance on *The Name of the Game*, but this time were seen backing actor Don Stroud lip-syncing to 'Pineapple Rose', also the episode's title in the opening scene. (This was after Stroud had fronted the Visions on *Run for Your Life*.) According to Randy Naylor on randymeisnerretrospective.com, "We had a couple of pretty cool tunes that were recorded just for these shows" (*Ironside* and *The Name of the Game*). The **Poor** released several excellent singles on the Loma, York and Decca labels but unfortunately never scored the success their music and high-profiles TV appearances should have warranted.

Despite their *Daniel Boone* cameo falling through, the **Lewis & Clarke Expedition** performed an otherwise unreleased song, 'Bring on the Sundown' on the December 30 episode of *I Dream of Jeannie*. They appeared in a wild party scene in Major Nelson's living room, with Major Healy joining in on the playing on a trashcan. The group recorded several singles for the Colgems and RCA labels in addition to their *Earth, Air, Fire & Water* album. Although quite popular in all the teen magazines and despite the backing of the Monkees' Michael Nesmith, the **Lewis & Clarke Expedition** fell short of expected stardom.

Closing out the year, on December 31, **Spanky & Our Gang** performed 'Yesterday's Rain' (Mercury 72871, November 1968) at a New Year's Eve party at the Ridgeville Country Club on *That's Life*. Flip Wilson, Mel Torme and Mort Sahl also entertained. As with all episodes from the series, this, too, is currently unavailable for viewing. As a result, the 'Sunday Will Never Be the Same' (Mercury 72679) and 'Like to Get to Know You' (Mercury 72795) band's line-up, which included at various times Geoffrey Meyers, John Seiter, Kenny Hodges, Lefty Baker, Malcolm Hale, Nigel Pickering, Oz Bach, and Elaine "Spanky" McFarlane, could not be identified.

10 p.m., Ch. 2. That's Life (color). Guests Mel Torme, Mort Sahl, Flip Wilson and Spanky and Our Gang join for an evening of merrymaking.

TV Guide listing for Spanky & Our Gang's appearance on *That's Life*. Clipping from the author's collection.

Also in 1968, the March 8 issue of *Go* reported that "the **American Breed** fly to Miami at the end of this month to begin filming a pilot for a possible television series to be produced by Bing Crosby Productions. The pilot involves the adventures of a jet setter who gets himself into dramatic situations as he travels from city to city. The **American Breed** revealed . . . that they would be the resident band on the projected series, with local groups appearing in each episode depending on where the particular episode was being filmed." It's unknown if the pilot was ever aired, but it's been confirmed that at least portions were filmed. The **American Breed's**, best known for 'Bend Me, Shape Me' (Acta 45-811), personnel included Gary Loizzo, Al Ciner, Charles "Chuck" Colbert, Jim Michalak, Lee Graziano, and Kevin Murphy.

1969

The final musical group to appear on *That's Life*, on January 28, in the "Our First Vacation" episode, were **Little Anthony & the Imperials**. Most fondly remembered for 'Tears on My Pillow' (End E-1027) and 'Goin' Out of My Head' (DCP 1119), they performed the song 'This is the Life'. Another episode unavailable for viewing, it's presumed the group lineup included Jerome "Little Anthony" Gourdine, Ernest Wright, Clarence "Wa-hoo" Collins, and Samuel "Sammy" Strain.

On February 5, ABC's "*Laugh-In* gone berserk" sketch comedy series (it was created by Ed Friendly and George Schlatter, the same team behind the Rowan and Martin hit) *Turn On* debuted but was axed after the pilot's airing due to viewer complaints that it was "dirty" and "vulgar". *TV Guide* quoted producer Digby Wolfe as claiming it was "a visual, comedic, sensory assault involving . . . animation, videotape, stop-action film, electronic distortion, computer graphics—even people". Some of those "people" included the **Monkees**, sans Peter Tork (who by this time had left the group), who filmed an appearance scheduled to air on March 12 that, to this day, has apparently never been seen.

The **Strawberry Alarm Clock** appeared in the unsold pilot episode of the sitcom *The Best Years* (aka *Walt's Girls*) starring Craig Stevens. Although the pilot was filmed in either 1967 or 1968, it was not broadcast until August 4, 1969. The **Strawberry Alarm Clock** portrayed a band named the Dungeons. According to member George Bunnell, the band only had a couple of lines, and played next-door neighbors to Stevens' character's three daughters. Like the **Strawberry Alarm Clocks'** appearance on *The Danny Thomas Hour*, this show is also unavailable for viewing. In addition to Bunnell, the presumed group lineup included Randy Seol, Mark Weitz, and Steve Bartek.

Monday Tips

Craig Stevens is featured in a pilot film, "The Best Years," as a widowed father of three young girls. The rock group Strawberry Alarm clock makes a guest appearance. Channel 42 at 7 p.m.

Newspaper TV listings for *The Best Years* pilot listed the Strawberry Alarm Clock's appearance. Clipping from the author's collection.

Another unidentified rock band was seen backing a blues singer in the "A Hard Case of the Blues", the October 26 episode of *The Name of the Game*. Although the band was seen frequently and throughout the episode (on stage, in the studio, and prancing about), they were not billed.

1970

"The Night They Raided Daddy's", the February 19 episode of Marlo Thomas sitcom *That Girl*, centered on a group named the **Blue Boys**. Ann (Marlo Thomas) and her father hired a musical group to perform at his restaurant to help sagging business. Although referred to as "The Little Blue Boys," they were billed onscreen as "**Blue Boys**." The episode featured Rayburn Wallace, Jeff Brock, and Joe Duckett as the **Blue Boys**. There was also a rather extended scene of what very likely is a legit band performing an instrumental at a competing restaurant, and a band referred to as "Groovers" that auditioned before the **Blue Boys** were hired.

The **Fifth Dimension** (Marilyn McCoo, Billy Davis, Jr., Florence LaRue, Ron Townson and Lamonte McLemore) performed a Burt Bacharach/Hal David song, 'One Less Bell to Answer', and Neil Sedaka/Howard Greenfield's 'The Puppet Man' (both from their *Portrait* album Bell Records, Bell-6045, 1970) on the "To Sing a Song of Murder" episode of *It Takes a Thief*, aired February 23. The episode involved a McCoo as "A singer-guitarist with a group who gets mixed up in a political plot."

MUSIC AND MURDER make for a discordant duet when members of The 5th Dimension guest star in "Sing A Song of Murder," on Channel 4's "It Takes A Thief," Monday at 6:30 p.m.

Thief Role Shows Another Side Of Fifth Dimension Singer Marilyn

Marilyn McCoo has always wanted to be an actress, but singing became her way of life. And as a member of the 5th Dimension musical group, it's been a busy one.

Then along came Channel 4's "It Takes a Thief" with a part that might have been written for her: a singer-guitarist with a group who gets mixed up in a political plot. The episode, "Sing a Song of Murder," airing Monday at 6:30 p.m. has Miss McCoo making professional dramatic debut in the role of frightened Marilyn Lee. Playing opposite "Thief" star Robert Wagner ... that's not a bad way to make an acting debut.

"You never know, in this crazy show business, when anything is going to happen," said Miss McCoo, wife of Billy Davis Jr., also in the singing group. "One big song ("Up, Up and Away") made us. Now this."

All of the 5th Dimension, Miss McCoo, Davis, Florence LaRue, Ron Townson and Lamonte McLemore, play dramatic roles and sing in the ABC drama. They also introduce two new songs, "One Less Bell to answer" with music by Burt Bacharach and lyrics by Hal David, and "The Puppet Man," music and lyrics by Neil Sedaka and Howard Greenfield.

Programs of Note on KBYU-FM This Week

"Adventures in Learning" is a daily invitation from DBYU-FM 88.9MNZ and the Brigham Young University Division of Continuing Education to listeners interested in participating in informative, non-credit courses by radio.

On Mondays, Richard O. Cowan of the Department of Religious Instruction discusses an aspect of LDS Church history. Tuesdays, Lanier Britsch of the F. Kent Nielsen of the Department of Physics discussed science and religion. Fridays Darwin L. Hayes of the Department of English presents a series on literature appreciation. Saturdays Reed H. Bradford of the Department of Sociology discusses "The Sensitive Line". "Adventures in Learning" continues twice daily-at 6:45 a.m. and 2:45 p.m. on KBYU-FM.

Utah's *The Daily Herald* detailed the Fifth Dimension's appearance on *It Takes a Thief*. Article from the author's collection.

Three bands appeared on the March 27 episode of *The Name of the Game* and yet not one received billing. Thankfully, two have been identified. Universal recording stars the **Yellow Payges** (Dan Hortter, Dan Gorman, Bob Barnes, and Donnie Dacus) were prominently featured in "Jenny Wilde Is Drowning", performing 'Follow the Bouncing Ball' (UNI 55192, December 1969). The band performed in a nightclub scene at The Psychedelic Daffodil and had a few close ups, including one of their drumhead on full display. The group **Juarez** received ample time as well performing their song 'Lauderdale Rain', which had been released on Decca Records (Decca 32665) the month prior. The third group—currently unidentified—was seen in passing as the camera panned through a nightclub as the police came crashing in. Unfortunately, they performed an unknown instrumental so currently can't be identified by the song.

The July 5–11, 1969, issue of *TV Guide* reported that "Don Kirshner is co-producing a new pilot with Ernie Pintoff, which will star (natch) a saddled singing group of three boys and a girl called the **Kowboys**. The hunt is on for 18–23-year-olds who can sing and ride." Apparently, the cast eventually included Owens Boomer Castleman (as Matthew) and Michael Martin Murphy (as Zak), Jamie Carr (as Sweetwater) and Joy Bang (as Smitty). The show, set after the Civil War, was reportedly broadcast by NBC on July 13, 1970. Kirshner, of course, was behind *The Monkees*. He and Jeff Barry provided the country rock songs, including one titled 'Civilization'. As previously documented, both Castleman and Martin Murphy were previously with the Lewis & Clarke Expedition.

Restless after the war — the Civil War — four teen-agers (three guys and a gal) run away from their former lives, meet in the Old West and promptly run into a stagecoach stickup, in the "Monday Theatre" colorcast of "The Kowboys" on Channel 2 July 13 at 7 p.m.

The four young people are Matthew (Boomer Castleman) an Eastern bank clerk; Zak (Michael Martin Murphey) a Confederate dischargee; Sweetwater (Jamie Carr) a fence-hating nature lover; and Smitty (Joy Bang) fugitive from a foundling home.

The Kowboys, as the four call themselves, thwart an attempt to rob a stagecoach carrying a Presidential proclamation that would give statehood to a territory tyranically ruled by Capt. Luther Walker (Edward Andrews). Captain Walker, undiscouraged, wines and dine the Kowboys while preparing his next move — bombing the stagecoach.

Also cast are Frank Welker as Clem, Guy Raymond as Hezekiah, Tom Reese as Beard, Alice Backes as Mrs. Oliver, Jim Boles as Luke, Ken O'Brien as Scar and Herb Vigran as bank vice-president.

Executive producers of "The Kowboys," produced by 20th Century-Fox, are Ernie Pintoff and Don Kirshner, with Pintoff directing from a script he wrote with Max Wilk.

FOUR YOUNG PEOPLE, converging from all directions on the Old West after the Civil War, team up in the "Monday Theatre" colorcast of "The Kowboys" on Channel 2 July 13 at 7 p.m. The four, from left, are Jamie Carr as Sweetwater, Boomer Castleman as Matthew, Joy Band as Smitty and Michael Martin Murphey as Zak.

SCANNING CHANNELS

The pilot for Don Kirshner's post-Monkees' group, the Kowboys, never made it to series. Article from the author's collection.

"The War Merchants", the October 30 episode of *The Name of the Game*, featured a three-man band (two guitars and drums) performing in a strip club behind a dancer. The group played an extended rock instrumental and was seen at the start of the scene as well as at the very end. They did not receive any billing.

Like Desi Arnaz's band (and whether they comprised real musicians or not) his sister Lucie (as Kim Carter), had her own band on *Here's Lucy*. On "Lucy and Rudy Vallée", aired November 30, her band performed the Beatles' "She Came in Through the Bathroom Window". Rudy Vallée, from the Golden Age of Hollywood, also took a stab at the song, prompting Kim to say, "I've never heard it sung quite that way before."

Well, hardly ever. Lucy thinks a "now" approach can revive the career of singer Rudy Vallee. Will today's audiences take to the hills? Or go for the Vallee?

HERE'S LUCY. 8:30 PM. CBS⑤5,12

Rudy Vallée becomes hip by joining a rock n' roll band on *Here's Lucy*. Ad from the author's collection.

According to the IMDB listing for the December 16 sitcom in a school *Room 222*, "Several students at Walt Whitman have formed a band, the Nickel-Plated Toothpick that has a shot at a recording contract with a Nashville record producer, thanks to the efforts of the band's manager, Sam Cousins, who operates a local discotheque. The band's lead guitarist, however, Mel Wertz, is deeply conflicted—his dream is to be a teacher but going forward with the recording contract and the required touring and publicity will mean missing that semester's finals—and perhaps giving up on his dream of being a teacher." Although the members of the Nickel-Plated Toothpick were not credited, IMDB lists the band (for performance and music) as **Moccasin**, so it's assumed it was a real group. Apparently, **Moccasin** did not have any record releases; internet searches come up empty.

Not to be confused with the Pearly Gate from *Judd for the Defense*, the group performing as the **Pearly Gates**, as was the norm for *The Name of the Game*, were not credited in the December 18 "The Glory Shouter" episode, so it's uncertain whether the group was a "real" band. They were seen in two different scenes: Once performing on the set of a religious TV program, and once performing at the Rose Bowl. On set, they performed an electric-countrified religious ditty, leading to Howard Duff referring to them as "electronic noisemakers" (he also noted the band was previously known by the name Evil Ways). Ron Dante (of the Archies) had a studio group named the Pearly Gates during the time this episode was filmed, but it's unlikely that this was his group.

While the 1960's might have popularized the rock group cameo, the strategy of featuring a band on an episode of a network television series to increase ratings or to even further plot has remained consistent in the ensuing decades. The Dickies on the Don Rickles' sitcom *C.P.O. Sharkey*, the Doobie Brothers on the classic sitcom *What's Happening!!*, Devo on the Sarah Jessica Parker sitcom *Square Pegs*, the Ramones *on The Simpsons*, the Flaming Lips on *Beverly Hills 90210*, and Sonic Youth on *Gossip Girl* are just some of many, many post-1960's appearances. Even current reality-based TV shows feature popular rock bands or music artists to promote a ratings spike; as a result, there's little doubt the trend will continue.

Appendix A: Fictitious Band Appearances

Capitalizing on the popularity of televised music performances, many 1960's TV series either featured their stars forming a rock and roll group or meeting up with a fictional band. Several of the episodes are incredibly laughable and often showcased how the older TV production teams took subtle knocks at youth culture by writing terribly unhip dialogue meant to be cool, or by presenting outlandish visuals—obviously phony wigs and/or loud costumes. Whether exaggerating performances or offering more accurate representations, several additional television programs grooved to a rock and roll beat . . . .

1964

Surprisingly, "The Combo" episode of *The Donna Reed Show* aired January 9—*before* the Beatles' *Ed Sullivan Show* appearance. Jeff Stone's band, the **Jeff Stone Combo**, was seen playing at a party and eventually decided to make a record. The show starred Paul Peterson, Darryl Richard, Jimmy Hawkins, and Gary Waynesmith. Their song, 'I Want to be Free', was not the Monkees song.

On April 29, Patty Lane introduced Bertram Bristol (aka Binky or "the Mop") to her school mates on *The Patty Duke Show's* "Leave it to Patty" episode. His group was an odd mixture of rockabilly and rock, and his song ("Open Up Your Heart", lyrics by Sidney Sheldon and music by Sid Ramin) started similarly to 'Twist & Shout' and included a punchy "Ooooohhhh". Binky was played by John Kenney, who closed the episode by repeating the song in the Lane's living room.

1965

"The Case of the Frustrated Folk Singer", from the January 7 *Perry Mason*, centered on the **Jazbo Williams Trio**, a Hollywood club band led by actor Gary Crosby. The band was seen throughout and backed folk singer Amy Jones Jennings (Bonnie Jones) at a coffee house for her rendition of 'Greensleeves' and 'Careless Love'.

Although not featured in the January 22 "The Hatrocks and the Gruesomes" episode of *The Flintstones*, the **4 Insects** appeared on a billboard promoting "Bug Music" at the World's Fair. Each of the head shots of the four members were drawn with exaggerated Beatles-like mop tops.

The pre-*Here's Lucy* program, *The Lucy Show*, featured "Lucy in the Music World". The September 27 episode highlighted Lucy's and Mel Torme's performance as the **Tear Ducts** on *The Wing Ding Show*. Another musical act that appeared was the **DDTs** ("a group that will do away with the Beatles"), a ridiculous looking band with striped shirts, long haired wigs, and large, phony plastic glasses.

The Man From U.N.C.L.E (or men from U.N.C.L.E, Napoleon Solo and Illya Kuryakin) investigated a THRUSH operation using a discotheque as a front in "The Discotheque Affair". In one scene in this October 25 episode, Kuryakin (played by David McCallum) played an upright bass in a combo.

A band led by Bobby Sherman (starring as Nicky Van) and including Michael J. Pollard dominated the plot of the "Princess & The Paupers" episode of *Honey West*, aired October 21. The **Paupers** opened the show performing a song possibly titled 'Mama Saw Me with My Girl' at the Club Nova. Sherman also sang another song at the end of the episode.

In addition to their episodes featuring cameo guest stars, *The Flintstones'* November 26 "The Masquerade Party" featured two faux groups: The **Way-Outs** (who performed 'Way Out') and the **Beasties**.

1966

Having decided against King Cobra and the Rattlers, Digit Dialing and the Busy Signals, and Admiral Dewey and the Permanent Waves, a pre-*Monkees* Davy Jones (billed as David Jones) was the leader of **Moe Hill & the Mountains** (also the episode's title). The group performed 'Gonna Buy Me a Dog' (again, not a Monkees version) while recording a demo on the January 7 *The Farmer's Daughter*. Also mentioned was a group named the Dumplings.

The **Gories** were a band created by the *Gidget* gang specifically for "Gidget's Career" on this January 20 episode. The band was seen rehearsing in Gidget's living room and performing on a live TV show (without Gidget). Interestingly, in the "Ring-A Ding-Dingbat" episode, aired February 24, Gidget got involved with a British Invasion duo named the **Dingbats**. And, in yet another episode ("All the Best Diseases are Taken", November 17, 1965), Gidget tried to book a guitar-playing beatnik-type (Henry Jaglom as Billy Roy Soames) for a performance. He was heard (but not seen) singing an acoustic snippet of the Gas Co.'s 'Blow Your Mind' (Mirwood 5501 A), a Screen Gems/Columbia Music release.

Stephen Baxter, also known as "My Son, The Sheepdog", formed the **Leaping Lizards** on the February 14 episode of *Hazel*. The group was seen rehearsing in a garage and appeared on TV on the *Pandemonium Rock 'N Roll Contest* which, of course, they won. The group performed only instrumentals and Baxter rocked out with his accordion. At one point, the **Lizards** even performed a little jump-step while playing but wind up completely out of step with each other! They rocked to 'Anteater Rock' and 'Hully Gully with Jelly'.

That same night, Chad & Jeremy appeared on *Batman* in "The Cat's Meow" playing themselves. Part of arch villain Catwoman's plan to steal the duo's voices involved forming her own rock group, **Catwoman and the Kittens**, with Eenie, Meanie, Miney and Mo.

On February 25, Marlene (Suzie Kaye), Biff (Rex Allen, Jr.), Freddie, and Leonard formed a band—the **Dropouts**—with the help of Tommy and Dick Smothers of *The Smothers Brothers Show* (aka *My Brother the Angel*). In "Heaven Help the Dropout", the group "played" various tunes, and was seen practicing, rehearsing, and performing. Locales played include the Flooded Cellar and Crane High School. Marlene frugged along to the band but did not actually play an instrument.

There was "A Singer in Town" as **Keevy Hazelton** arrived in Mayberry with his rock band and performed a rock version of Aunt Bee's song, 'My Hometown' on the April 11 *The Andy Griffith Show*. With go go chicks, Ron Howard as Opie frugging, and a '60's TV dance show . . . .

Much like the Bed Bugs, the **Tomahawk Trio** (although not played by an actual band) performed a wild rockin' instrumental that musically fell way outside the immediate post-Civil War-era setting on *F Troop*. On the April 26 "Lieutenant O'Rourke, Front and Center" episode, the Playbrave Club, complete with Playbrave Squirrels dancing in short Native American dresses, go-go danced to the three-member group. The **Tomahawk Trio** proved so popular that they were "held over four weeks at Little Bighorn."

Although heard but not seen, **Benedict Arnold & the Traitors'** album had Bruce Wayne's Aunt Harriet (Madge Blake) groovin' to 'The Catusi', "the latest dance" that started at the Pink Sandbox on the September 14 "Hot Off the Griddle" episode of *Batman*. Dick Grayson (Burt Ward) was less enthusiastic, proclaiming, "Oh boy. I like rock and roll music as much as the next red-blooded average American teenager, but this stuff is awful." The Pink Sandbox featured wild cage go-go dancing and loud music but, unfortunately, no band.

As a show about a small-time local Los Angeles rock group, episodes of *The Monkees* were bound to feature competing bands. The October 3 "Your Friendly Neighborhood Kidnappers" featured the **Four Swines**, a leather-clad group dressed like bikers who were shown playing an instrumental.

The "On the Flip Side" episode of *ABC Stage 67*, aired on December 7, featured the **Celestials**. Per *TV Guide*, it was "an original musical with a rock and roll beat. Singer Charles O'Conner is entering old age (he's 25) and his career is on the decline. Heaven help poor Charles! It does: A hard rock quartet drops out of the clear blue sky to help Charles modernize his sound for the 'in' crowd. Burt Bacharach and Hal David songs include 'It Doesn't Matter Anymore', 'Fender Mender', and 'Take a Broken Heart'. Starring Ricky Nelson." The **Celestials** were played by Joanie Sommers, Tyrone Cooper, Steve Perry, and Jeff Siggins.

1967

"Find the Monkees", the January 23 episode of *The Monkees* that revolved around a TV producer who invited several local bands to an audition, featured the **Foreign Agents** (three members dressed in black spy trench coats); the **Four Martians**, seen in red and gold costumes typical of science fiction shows of the era . . . except with pantyhose on their heads; and the **Jolly Green Giants**, three members that looked as if they stepped off of a frozen vegetables can.

Created by Sherwood Schwartz, the man behind *Gilligan's Island*, sitcom *It's About Time* revolved around a cave family that was somehow brought to the future by a pair of astronauts. In this episode, the cast formed a band (playing buckets, pots, pans, and sink pipes) and rocketed to success based on their song, 'Dinosaur Stew'. Not only did the song reach #1 on the charts, but the band appeared on *The Fred Gulliver Show* causing havoc for some ballerinas. Recording for Big Beat Records, they met a "real" band, the **Apes**, which featured a very young Karen Valentine (later a star of *Room 222*). "Cave Family Swingers" aired on August 13. The Beatles, Sonny and Cher, and the King Family are mentioned along with other faux bands Morris the Missionary and the Four Cannibals, Harry Hands and His Four Fingers, and Dick the Dentist and His Four Cavities.

An unconfirmed rumor has it that the **Sound Committee** was Opie actor Ron Howard's real band but it's doubtful. On *The Andy Griffith Show*, "Opie's Group" (Gary Chase as Jesse Clayton, Jim Kidwell as Clifford Johnson, and Joe Leitch as Wilson Brown) was also the name of the episode, which aired November 6. The teen band performed a cool instrumental in the living room at a teen party and was also seen rehearsing.

Featuring an appearance by Jeremy Clyde—one half of Chad & Jeremy—*My Three Sons'* "Liverpool Saga", which aired December 23, featured Chip's (one of the titular "three sons" as portrayed by Stanley Livingston) band, **Chip Douglas and the Dynamiters**. Needing help to win a battle of the bands, Chip called Clyde's character. The **Dynamiters** were seen numerous times throughout the episode, primarily in the Douglas' living room. The band was also seen performing—and winning—the battle on stage in a teen club. Songs included 'Greensleeves' and an unknown instrumental. One of the other bands that the **Dynamiters** competed against was briefly shown finishing their song.

1968

Yet another fake group appeared on *The Monkees'* March 4 "Some Like it Lukewarm" episode. To win Jerry 'The Geator with the Heator' Blavat's (an authentic TV and radio host) KXIW Rock-athon contest, Davy dressed in drag while Daphne, a member of the **West-Minstrel Abbies**, dressed as a man.

Unlike the Raspberry Watchband—portrayed by the Sundowners—the **Banana Wristwatch** was a fictitious group on the May 12 comedy sketch program *The Carol Burnett Show*. Unavailable for viewing, listings describe the skit as "a satire of a Rock 'n Roll band".

The Saturday morning favorite *The Banana Splits* were introduced on an NBC Saturday Morning Preview special that aired in prime time on September 6. *Kellogg's Presents The Banana Splits Adventure Hour* debuted the following morning. During the preview, Fleegle, a dog guitar player (Jeff Winkless aka Jeffrey Brock), Drooper, a lion guitarist (Dan Winkless aka Daniel Owen), Bingo, the gorilla drummer (Terence H. Winkless aka Terence Henry) and Snorky, the elephant keyboard player (Robert Towers) performed 'You're the Lovin' End'. The Banana Splits also hosted the 1969 preview, but it aired on August 30 during normal Saturday morning hours.

The opening scene of the October 10 "Tiger by the Tail" episode of *Hawaii Five-O* featured a Hawaiian band (wearing Hawaiian shirts) backing Sal Mineo while he performed 'Ain't No Big Thing', which he performed on the stage of The Swinger club.

1969

The most ridiculous documented fictitious group of them all would be **Blue Boy Roy and the Electric Zoo**. The January 29 *The Beverly Hillbillies* episode stared country musician Roy Clark in one of his three appearances as Roy Halsey (Cousin Roy). "Cousin Roy in Movieland" featured Clark in a Buster Brown suit and wig performing the Platters' 'The Great Pretender'. A monkey joined in on tambourine and a bear contributed drums.

On *Family Affair*, in "The Flip Side", aired March 24, child actor and singer Eddie Hodges played a singer that Cissy fell in love with—only to be done wrong by. The name of Eddie's group was **Charlie & the Unsung Heroes**, and, in fact, the full group (three guitars, sax and drums) appeared at the start of the episode but only on a TV screen. Hodges recalled that "the band was composed of actors and were not a real band. We went into the studio to record both 'Cissy My Love' (which Eddie performed solo) and another song I performed with the 'band' called 'I Think of Her', which was written by my writing partner at the time, Tandyn Almer. As I recall, I called in some friends for that session; one, I think, was Larry Duncan."

Though conceived as a cartoon, each episode of *The Hardy Boys* series featured live-action clips of a real rock band modeled to look like their cartoon characters and who solved mysteries. A Saturday morning show, a total of twenty four episodes were broadcast in 1969, with the premier debuting on September 6. The *1969 ABC Saturday Morning Cartoon Preview*, aired September 4, was a prime time TV special previewing ABC's Saturday morning cartoon line-up. Framed by the cast of *The Ghost & Mrs. Muir*, the special featured the first live action clips from *The Hardy Boys*. Reed Kailing played Frank, Jeff Taylor played Joe, Bob Crowder starred as Pete, Nibs Soltysoak was Chubby and Deven English portrayed Wanda Kay. Two members were from authentic '60's bands—the Destinations (Kailing) and the Messengers (Taylor).

The Hardy boys (yes, guys, the one on the left is a girl) are alive and kicking and animated, too. It could only happen in Hollywood.

New Detective Series

Saturday morning, on television, is another world. Norman Prescott is a Saturday morning expert. He heads up, with Lou Scheimer and Hal Sutherland, Filmation, the animation studio that turned out series, like Superman, Batman, Aquamand and the big hit, Archie. This year, on ABC, will come another Filmation series, The Hardy Boys.

The Hardy Boys (yes, guys, the one on the left is a girl) are alive and kicking and animated, oto. It could only happen in Hollywood.

Prescott says that the Saturday morning audience is made up of people between the ages of two and 14. That limits, strictly, what can be done. You can't animate Dostoevsky for two-year-olds.

The Hardy Boys will be a detective series—but non-violent, in keeping with the current fad—and The Hardy Boys will also sing rock 'n' roll, between clues.

In fact, a real, live group called The Hardy Boys has been assembled. They will make personal appearances and do television guest shots and make records.

Prescott's animators created the characters for The Hardy Boys (there is one girl among the Boys, which could only happen in Hollywood) and then the casting department went out and found singers who looked like the five drawings.

Although a Saturday morning program, the *Hardy Boys* debuted in prime time. Article from the author's collection.

1970

The Ray Stevens Show was a mixture of music and skit-based comedy. In addition to featuring real groups such as the Guess Who and the Lettermen, former Mamas and Papas singer Cass Elliot fronted the fictional **Mitzi & the Polkadots**. Elliott appeared in several episodes and appeared with the **Polkadots** in at least the July 11 show.

The September 20 episode of *Mission Impossible*, titled 'Flip Side', featured a brief scene of Lesley Ann Warren backed by a three-piece combo (guitar, drums, and piano) while singing on stage. The guitarist was played by *Star Trek's* Leonard Nimoy, lending credence to this being a fictitious group.

The royal family of all fictitious groups had to be the *Partridge Family*. Modeled after the real-life hit makers ('The Rain, The Park, and Other Things', 'Indian Lake', and 'Hair') the Cowsills, the sitcom debuted on September 25 and ran for ninety-six episodes. The group, of course, regularly performed on the show and scored a series of bubble gummy pop hits in the first half of the decade. David Cassidy, Shirley Jones, Susan Dey, Danny Bonaduce, Suzanne Crough, and Jeremy Gelbwaks (and, later, Brian Forster) all became huge TV stars behind the magic of producer Wes Farrell, the Ron Hicklin Singers, and the Wrecking Crew.

There was an unknown band appearance in the *Ironside* episode "Noel's Gonna Fly" (aired October 15). Tim Considine played the guitarist, so it's very possible it was a group comprised of other actors. The band was seen several times throughout the episode.

An odd episode of *The Name of the Game* filmed as a Greek Chorus ("All the Old Familiar Faces", aired November 13) featured a group named the **Third Eye** performing several songs, including "All the Old Familiar Faces". The combo (Alyce Andrece, Rhea Andrece, James J. Joyce, Jon Joyce, and Randy Joyce) only sang and did not perform any instruments, so it's unknown whether they were a real singing group, but considering they appeared to combine two sets of families it's possible they were.

Appendix B: Game Shows and Other Appearances

1965

The popular game show *The Dating Game* (ABC-TV) often times featured celebrities (some prior to finding fame) and/or musicians as contestants. It premiered December 20 during afternoon hours with the **Regents** (Craig Boyd, Jerry Rosa, John Harris, Johnny Mann and Mike McDonald), who initially performed the theme song, as house band guesting for at least the debut show (and likely longer). The **Regents** were a very popular Los Angeles-area band that had already recorded a live album (*The Regents at the A.M.–P.M. Discotheque*) on Capitol Records prior to their appearances, and released a 45 on Reprise (0430) around the time of the premiere. In 1966, a prime time version of *The Dating Game* broadcast in color premiered. Beginning in 1967, musical guests would first perform an edited song with their group, while a member or two would then compete in the game. Bands that appeared included the **Merry-Go-Round**, the **Gene Clark Group**, the **Grass Roots**, the **Buckinghams**, **Iron Butterfly**, **Strawberry Alarm Clock**, **Wadsworth Mansion**, **Tommy James & the Shondells**, **Dino, Desi & Billy**, the **Clique**, **Every Mother's Son**, and **Don & the Goodtimes**. Other musical acts that appeared included **Mama Cass**, the **Irish Rovers**, the **Stampeders**, the **Hollies** and **Little Anthony & the Imperials**; Bobby Fuller (**Bobby Fuller Four**), Dewey Martin (**Buffalo Springfield**), Terry Knight (**the Pack**), **Maurice** and **Robin Gibb** (Bee Gees), **Dusty Springfield** and **Mark Lindsay** (**Paul Revere and the Raiders**) apparently appeared as contestants. There were undoubtedly others.

Los Angeles' the Regents were the house band for the initial season of *The Dating Game*. Photo from the author's collection.

1966

I've Got a Secret, where a panel of celebrities tried to guess a contestants secret by asking pointed questions, premiered in 1952 and often times featured musical acts. In fact, surf band the Cornells turned up in 1963 and performed 'Caravan.' In 1966, however, during the height of rock n' roll's "invasion" on television, a band named the **Live Wires**, appeared on January 17. The group performed the instrumental '900 Miles.' Their secret? A member was the son of Durwood Kirby, a popular radio and television celebrity best known for *The Gary Moore Show* and *Candid Camera*.

The **Hi-5**, whose secret was they agreed to get "normal" haircuts after their appearance on *I've Got a Secret*, performed 'Did You Have To Rub It In' on the March 7 episode.

Tony & the Tigers performed an almost unrecognizable version of Lennon-McCartney's 'I'll Be On My Way' on the September 26 *I've Got a Secret*. The group included John Meredith, John Pusetdart, and Hunt and Tony Fox Sales, two of comedian Soupy Sales' sons.

While not necessarily a scripted show, and much like today's so-called reality TV, *Candid Camera* created predetermined skits that outlined their performers' actions. The November 20 episode of the hidden camera comedy swayed a bit from the customary format and featured teen band the **Mods** (Rich Lillie, vocals and guitar; Bob Busch, bass; Phil Watson, lead guitar; Bruce Cunningham, drums; Bob Lillie, guitar; and Wally Hageman, guitar) from Monmouth County, New Jersey performing a song they composed titled, 'Smile, You're on Candid Camera' (Mod Records DC 116, written by Ray Dayrouge and Sam Siciliano). According to Allen Funt's brief intro, the group had contacted the show requesting to play the song and was provided permission. This is the same **Mods** group that recorded the all-time classic garage rock song, 'Ritual' (Revelation VII 105).

On another similar game show, *To Tell the Truth*, where contestant tried to identify imposters by, again, asking pointed questions, Native American rock group the **Chieftones** performed 'Do Lord' on December 26.

1967

Although the air date could not be determined, *Candid Camera* again welcomed a rock group and featured an appearance by the **Four Seasons** (Frankie Valli, Bob Gaudio, Tommy DeVito, and Nick Massi). The group was seen rehearsing "their latest hit" ('Beggin', Philips 404332, February 1967) in a high school, as unsuspecting schoolgirls outside the room excitedly reacted to the group being there.

1968

The pilot for the prime time game show *The Generation Gap* was filmed in 1968 and featured the **Turtles**. The object of the Dennis

Wholey-hosted program was for contestants under the age of thirty to compete against those over the age of thirty. The series actually premiered February 7, 1969, this time featuring the **Ohio Express** performing 'Yummy, Yummy, Yummy' (Buddah BDA 38). The program lasted sixteen episodes (and replaced Wholey with Jack Barry during the course of its run). Other rock groups to appear included **Tommy James & the Shondells, 1910 Fruitgum Co.,** the **Classics IV,** the **Brooklyn Bridge, Jay & the Americans, Gladys Knight & the Pips, Joey Dee & the Starlighters,** and the **Peppermint Rainbow.** Barbara and Bob Cowsill, of the **Cowsills,** appeared as contestants.

Index